Praise 1

MW00439186

"Many Christians who start well do not continue well, and some who continue for a while do not finish well. The burden of this book is from a man who was used by God to grow an exciting and fruitful church in San Antonio for more than thirty years, and after that is traveling the world encouraging leaders and pastors. This practical book is not just about techniques for keeping on, but recognizes the key to stability and growth is Jesus Christ himself, who lives within his people and is Himself the source of their strength and wisdom. As you read the many stories in this book you keep bumping into Jesus, for the lives that have made any spiritual impact have only one explanation, it was "not I, but Christ." This could change your life too!"

—Charles Price, Senior Pastor, The Peoples Church, Toronto, Canada

"Steve and I have worked together in a number of evangelistic campaigns and missions events these past two decades. He is a good friend and brother. He has a tremendous passion for missions, evangelism, and the local church. Steve is a man of God, faithful servant leader, and champion for the great commission. He is one of the most qualified people I know to minister to pastors, mission leaders, and their families. I enthusi-astically recommend the work of Shepherds' Support, Inc."

—*Luis Palau, international evangelist*

"Steve Troxel has been given a great gift, the gift of communicating God's Word to us. He uses this gift as well as anyone I know. He does so without ownership. He does so with great ease, wisdom, and humility. His views are firmly planted on the Bible, never adding and never taking away. Steve walks in the will of God and has helped change lives…including my own. I pray that you will go the distance in Christ's name."

—*Brian Anderson, television play-by-play announcer for the Milwaukee Brewers*

"Steve Troxel is the best! I have grown up in the church, lived all over the world, attended/joined numerous churches of many denominations from small to mega-church and I can attest he is the best preacher and pastor I have ever known. His understanding of the Bible and God's teachings is second to none. He always preaches the Gospel message and touches the hearts of all his listeners. Just as importantly, he lives what he preaches, and his life and Connie's reflect their love for the Lord and each other. As they expand their ministry to the rest of the world, they are truly taking on the Great Commission. The world will be a better place because the Troxels are making this move and taking God's love to the far reaches of our planet."

—*Richard "Tex" Brown, Lieutenant General (Ret), USAF*

"I have known Steve for nearly three decades now. He has been a great inspiration to me and my family as a man who earnestly seeks God's will. The same is true of his wife, Connie. Her love for God and support for Steve are an inspiration to him, as well as those of us who know them. As a teacher, Steve is true to God's Word. From the pulpit, he has been a model of truth, consistency, and integrity. As a friend, he models that same truth, consistency, and integrity. God's Word is written, and is still being written, on Steve's heart, and he has a heart that wants to share it with all."

—*Burt Hooton, former major league baseball pitcher and current pitching coach*

"Steve is a dynamic shepherd with a tender heart for pastors, third world ministries, and a sincere love that exceeds racial boundaries. My ministry has been richly blessed because of our intimate personal and spiritual relationship, global travel experiences, and pulpit exchanges. His ministry epitomizes the great commission."

—*Rander Draper, senior pastor of Maranatha Bible Church in San Antonio, Texas*

"Steve is a proven pastor, a great Bible teacher, and a man of integrity. He has been a blessing to my life personally, and I believe that God is going to use him in the years to come to encourage and strengthen pastors around the world with his solid biblical teaching. Pastor Troxel is a pastor's pastor. His thirty-four years of shepherding Wayside Chapel in San Antonio has made him a man who knows the victories and struggles that the pastor faces."

—*Sammy Tippit, international evangelist*

"Steve is a true pioneer, passionate visionary, and pastor to pastors for so many. Only eternity will reveal how far reaching, how life transforming, how world impacting Steve's leadership has been at the helm of Wayside. Now as he devotes his efforts to be a full-time encouragement to those engaged in ministry around the world, God will be glorified even more through this man after His own heart. I consider it a privilege to know Steve and to commend him to you."

—*Rob Harrell, Senior Pastor of First Evangelical Free Church in Austin, Texas*

"During my thirty-eight years as a missionary and missions leader, I have not met anyone as effective in building up and encouraging national pastors as Steve. His ability to speak to the life and ministry issues faced by pastors grows out of his own years of experience as a senior pastor coupled with an unpretentious transparency of life. Having served closely with him for over a decade on his pastoral staff, I was able to observe that his life backs up what he preaches."

—*Marvin Smith (deceased), former missionary and Missions Pastor at Wayside Chapel in San Antonio, Texas*

"Tom Landry, legendary coach of the Dallas Cowboys, was once asked to define what a coach does. Landry replied, 'A coach is a man who gets men to do what they don't want to do, so that they can become what they've always wanted to be.' As the pastor who was privileged to follow Steve here at Wayside Chapel, I can say that Steve fulfilled the role of not only a coach, but also that of a gentle shepherd as he fed and led his flock. I feel fortunate to benefit not just from Steve's past investment in the kingdom but also his ongoing ministry of 'iron sharpening iron' as he builds into the lives of leaders, including mine. I am excited that others, who may never meet Steve personally, will benefit from his coaching through this book as he encourages us to keep running the race as servant leaders."

—*Roger Poupart, senior pastor at Wayside Chapel Evangelical Free Church in San Antonio, Texas*

GOING THE DISTANCE

GOING THE DISTANCE
LIFE'S A MARATHON, NOT A SPRINT
by STEPHEN P. TROXEL

TATE PUBLISHING & Enterprises

Published by Tate Publishing & Enterprises, LLC
127 E. Trade Center Terrace | Mustang, Oklahoma 73064 USA
1.888.361.9473 | www.tatepublishing.com

Tate Publishing is committed to excellence in the publishing industry. The company reflects the philosophy established by the founders, based on Psalm 68:11,
"The Lord gave the word and great was the company of those who published it."

Book design copyright © 2008 by Tate Publishing, LLC. All rights reserved.
Cover design by Jacop Crissup
Interior design by Kandi Evans

Published in the United States of America

ISBN: 978-1-60696-327-2

1. Christian Living: Spiritual Growth: General

2. Church & Ministry: Pastoral Helps: Pastoral Care
08.08.06

DEDICATION

I dedicate this book to those who know me the best, love me the most, and who have tolerated so much.

I am forever indebted to my dad and mom, Robert and Isabel Troxel, whose faith was simple but firm to the very end. They both died early: Mom in 1963 and Dad in 1978. First John 5:13 is engraved on their tombstone: "These things I have written to you who believe in the name of the Son of God, that you may know that you have eternal life, and that you may continue to believe in the name of the Son of God" (NKJV). The imprint of their lives can be seen all over me. It is part of both my physical and spiritual DNA.

My wife, Connie, and I have two daughters, Shelli and Kelli, and one son-in law, Don Johnson (a man of integrity), along with six grandchildren, who have encouraged me along the way and nourished my soul. Both daughters have been a father's delight. We have spent many enjoyable vacations together with Don and Kelli and their children, which have brought refreshment to my soul when most needed. Shelli's journey has been more difficult, but she too is a daughter of faith.

I have a sister, Rita, and a brother-in-law, Dr. Dale Economan, who is a physician in Marion, Indiana.

In so many ways, our lives have paralleled theirs with the medical profession and the ministry sharing many things in common. They too have encouraged me during difficult times. We have prayed for one another, cried at times, and laughed together as close family members will and should.

My brother Jed and his wife, Karen, are delightful to be around. Jed likes restoring old things like cars, trucks, tractors, boats, and, well, you name it, he does it well. As I write these words, he is finishing the restoration of a 1959 Ford convertible. In ministry, we are about restoring lives. I have seen patience in him and a simple conviction that life is to be lived in the present, not worrying about the future.

My in-laws, Darrell and Beulah Hyde, have been my surrogate parents for years. God took Darrell home in the spring of 2006. Mom and sweet Larry, Connie's brother (who is mentally challenged), have lived with us since the fall of 2000. Larry teaches us patience and brings us to a much needed slower pace at times. I have been encouraged much by Mom. She is so generous, so joyful and full of life. At the age of ninety-two, she is still a pleasure to be around. She recently picked up her mouth organ again, and we hear joyful music coming from her end of the house. You will hear no complaints from her side and no mother-in-law jokes from ours. She is one who is aging gracefully and finishing well.

And of course, my lovely bride, Connie, has been there since the day we pledged our love to one another: July 1, 1962. We have been privileged to minister side by side all over the world during our years together, and though we have sung together many times, I still most love to hear her sweet, exquisite, solo voice. Part of her testimony that she shares with the women in pastors' wives conferences in other countries is about how difficult the journey has been for us. Although it hasn't been easy, I would not have wanted it any other way because she has been by my side. She is a woman of faith.

We look forward to the duration of our journey together, and we both want to finish strong the course God has for us.

ACKNOWLEDGMENTS

I am greatly indebted to several people for helping me get this project off the ground and to the publisher. First of all, I am indebted to my grandson, Derek Johnson, for taking time out of his busy schedule as an honors student at Texas A&M University, to format this book before it was sent to the publisher. I owe much to Derek, who has been a great source of joy and pride for his entire family. Thank you, Derek, for who you are and what you are capable of doing. We believe that the sky is the limit for you.

Many thanks also go to John Shields, attorney at law, for the colossal amount of work and energy he has put into making sure that our new ministry was operating within the law and the IRS guidelines for a 5013c (nonprofit) organization when we started Shepherds' Support Inc. (SSI). John has been a ready legal mind to help in time of need. He also took the time to read this entire manuscript in its raw version and make invaluable suggestions, which were for the most part included in the final product. Thank you, John, for caring so much about the Lord's work and paying attention to the details.

I also want to thank our entire Shepherds' Support

Board consisting of John and Marsha Shields, Doctors Keith and Beth Eyre, Lannie and Melba Green, and Dr. Glen and Marilyn Mott. They have been most supportive of this project and have allowed me the time (which I totally underestimated) to see it through to completion. Thank you, my SSI colleagues, for caring so much about equipping and encouraging pastors and wives everywhere and allowing Connie and me the luxury of serving in this manner.

I also thank Diana Lowe, my administrative assistant, who has been a gift from God to our ministry. Her help in taking care of so many details has freed me up to spend more time in ministry and to accomplish projects such as this one. She and her husband Rick, missions and outreach pastor at Wayside Chapel, both read the manuscript and made many helpful suggestions and corrections.

Next, I want to thank two friends, both busy senior pastors of large churches and ministries, who took the time to read the manuscript. First, I want to thank Max Lucado, for writing an endorsement for this book. I have ministered with Max at two local men's gatherings, and I have witnessed myself his love for the Word and for God's people. The time constraints and demands upon Max are enormous. The fact that he was willing to take the time to read this manuscript (with many such requests that come his way) speaks volumes about his servant's heart and humility. Thanks, Max, for all that you do for so many. I am humbled that the "many" includes me.

Next, I want to thank my English friend Charles price, now the senior pastor at the Peoples Church in Toronto, Canada. I too have been privileged to minister alongside of him in a conference. I love to hear him open the Word. He blessed our church on many occasions during my time there. He is on TV in fifty-some countries and travels the world, presenting the indwelling life of Christ. I am honored that Charles would take the time and effort. Thanks Charles for the blessing that you are to the body of Christ throughout the world and for "remembering" me.

Finally, I want to thank my wife, Connie, for allowing our computer/study room to remain in disarray (like a war zone in her eyes) while this project was being finished. She too was part of the final editing crew as she took the time to read the manuscript and make valuable suggestions. Thanks, "Dear"; you are the best.

TABLE OF CONTENTS

INTRODUCTION

"You were thirty-four years in one pastorate. How did you do it?" I hear that question over and over again wherever Connie (my wife of forty-six years) and I go. How did we stay in the race when the going got tough? We know one thing: we didn't do it alone. We had plenty of help along the way.

I was a sprinter in high school, winning the 100-yard dash in our county during my last three years. I won the 220-yard dash each of the last two years of school. I liked to run fast, but not far. When the coach made us run a mile, I began to think physical abuse. I had an aversion to running far, but fast I could handle. Many approach the ministry as they would a 100-yard dash, but we need to think marathon. Any marathon runner will tell you that you need the help of others along the way to provide nourishment, refreshment, water, and just plain encouragement. "You can do it. Stay with it! Don't give up."

The purpose of this book is to provide encouragement to you for your spiritual marathon. You can finish the race that God has for you. My life verse has been Acts 20:24. Paul was on his way to Jerusalem. He met with the elders from the church at Ephesus. He knew that his immediate future was not very promising, to say the least. In verse 23 he says, "The Holy Spirit testifies in every city, saying that chains and tribulations await me" (NKJV). So much for positive thinking! He was thinking realistically. And he could say, "But none of these things move me; nor do I count my life dear to myself, so that I may finish my race with joy, and the ministry which I received from the Lord Jesus, to testify to the gospel of the grace of God" (Acts 20:24, NKJV).

The older I get, the more that verse has given clarity to my thinking. I desire to finish the race God has for me, and I plan to be running, not crawling, when I cross that line. I have always desperately needed and continue to need the help of others.

This book is interwoven in two major parts: the odd numbered chapters are on people who have helped us run, some of them not even realizing the impact that they have had on our lives. I have limited them to people who have been my contemporaries, even those older than me, who have finished well, and I concentrate on those who have impacted my life in my adult years. They will not be listed in any prioritized or chronological order.

The even numbered chapters are on passages from the Word that have influenced me and encouraged me to keep running. People and the Word: these are the only two entities that are eternal. Funny that they would be the two greatest influences in my life.

With that said, on to the main course. I hope you enjoy and find encouragement in my introducing you to some remarkable people and passages to spur you on to the finish.

CHAPTER ONE

MEET MARIA—A WOMAN OF PRAYER

BURNOUT

Meet Maria, all three-and-one-half feet of her. She is small in physical stature, deformed in appearance, but imposing in her spiritual stature. We first met Maria in October of 1997. Maria lives in Romania. I was just coming through one of the most difficult times in my personal life. Issues had knocked the spiritual wind right out of me. I had heard pastors and other Christian leaders speak about spiritual burnout but tended to downplay it as something that could never happen to "mature" Christians. And then, bam, I was smack dab in the middle of a spiritual and emotional pit.

I had lost my passion, and my feelings were frayed. I was just going through the motions, and those closest to me knew it. Dr. Richard Swenson, the doctor who wrote the book Margin,[1] just happened to be coming to Wayside Chapel (our home church of which I was senior pastor for thirty-four years) on my last weekend before a two-month sabbatical. We, along with the local chapter of the Christian-Medical-Dental Society (CMDS), hosted the good doctor for a weekend seminar. He spoke about burnout. All at once the lights came on, and I realized that was me. I was in a pit. How could I get out?

I considered dropping out of the race. Thoughts of getting out of the ministry were running relentlessly through my mind. I felt that God had removed His hand of blessing. I was washed up. It was time to hang up my running shoes and do something else.

I remember a funeral that I was conducting at the time. I was so distracted in my thoughts that I committed what seemed to be the unpardonable sin. Pastors almost always are to follow the lead car to the cemetery followed by the hearse and the family and the rest of the entourage. We were on a local freeway in the far right-hand lane, going about thirty-five miles per hour and about halfway to the cemetery when the thought came to me, Why is this car in front of me going so slow? I stepped on the accelerator, moved into the middle lane and proceeded to go around the lead car. As I came up parallel to the lead car, my wife brought me back to reality. She exclaimed, "Dear [always our term of endearment to each other], what are you doing?" I looked to my right to see the funeral director looking at me, with perhaps similar sentiments: Man, what are you doing? I braked and slipped back into line.

Remember the Southwest Airline commercials

where someone did something stupid like that? The commercials always end with the line, "Do you want to get away?" That was me.

I knew that it was time for me to get away.

God directed my thoughts to Psalm 40:1–3, which I had memorized many years ago. It reads:

> I waited patiently for the LORD; and He inclined to me, and heard my cry. He also brought me up out of a horrible pit, out of the miry clay, and set my feet upon a rock, and established my steps. He has put a new song in my mouth—praise to our God; many will see it and fear, and will trust in the Lord.
>
> Psalm 40:1–3 (NKJV)

I began to cry out daily for deliverance and a new song to be put in my mouth. They were slow in coming.

As we neared the latter half of our two-month sabbatical, we spent a month with our younger daughter and son-in-law, Kelli and Don Johnson, who were living on the eastern side of Italy for eighteen months. Don's business at the time had taken him there.

There was a memorable moment for me when we were standing on a mountaintop outside of Ascoli Piceno, looking down at several different shepherds tending their flocks of sheep grazing on the hillsides.

Something clicked inside of me. It was quiet. All we could hear was the blowing of the wind. This was the life of David. He had plenty of time to contemplate, to meditate, and to commune with God. No wonder so many of these great psalms came from the pen of this ready writer.

My world had become too noisy, too busy, and too crowded. I was allowing all of these distractions to keep me from communicating with the Creator, and I was running out of time. I had to make a decision. My daughter asked me one day, "Dad, are you ready to start preaching again?" I remember my answer to her: "I am not sure."

You see, there was one small problem. We were scheduled to leave Italy, go on to Switzerland by train, link up with our missionary friends Mike and Kathy, and then travel by car all the way across Austria, Hungary, and Transylvania, to the city of Bucharest. I was scheduled to be the keynote speaker for the Baptist Association of Pastors and Missionaries in Romania. There were to be 1,200 in attendance. It was almost panic time. What could I say? Could I really be honest? Would I just go through the motions? Nobody there really knows me, but those men have suffered much for their faith under Communism. I have suffered nothing for my faith. What in this world do I have to offer them? Scattered and fearful thoughts ran through my mind.

MEETING MARIA

And then little Maria entered our lives. From Bucharest, we had taken a three-hour train ride farther east and south to the city of Braila. We were staying at the home of Pastor Joseph and Mia Stefanutzi. We had a long-term relationship with them, and Wayside Chapel funded the construction of a new church building that was state of the art for the time and place. This little lady, Maria, stayed in the shadows, blending into the woodwork of the pastor's home. She was quietly serving in the kitchen, preparing delicious meals for us. I was intrigued by her size and her demeanor. I wanted to meet her, so Pastor Joseph had her come out. He introduced her as Mia's aunt. As she stood next to us, with her chin nearly resting on the table, we communicated with her through Pastor Joseph's translation. She began to pour out her heart to us. Tears filled her eyes as she spoke of her love for the Lord Jesus and her passion for all of Eastern Europe. She was seventy-five years of age at that time. She had lived under Communism all of her adult years, but her concern now was that with all of the newfound freedom, people would no longer see their need for God. They would throw their lives into materialism.

I will never forget what she said that day. She said, "I want to live as long as I can so I can pray for the people of Eastern Europe. I live to pray. When I heard that you were coming to visit us, I began to pray for you. I am praying for you every day. I will pray for you every day for the rest of my life. I will be praying for you as you go and speak at the conference."

This moment was a turning point for me. I knew that I had a prayer warrior by my side for the rest of her life. Where would I be without Maria? I shudder to think where. I will tell you later what happened at the conference.

OUR LAST MEETING WITH MARIA

In October of 2006, we conducted a pastors' wives seminar in Braila. Little Maria rode on a train all night, over twelve hours, to be there, mainly just to see us again, but also to be with her extended family. She was a breath of fresh air, a sweet aroma, a life-giving perfume.

In the process of our reunion, she confided that she had never missed a day praying for us since 1997. She also disclosed that she visits two or three families in her village every day, just to encourage them. I dread the day that God takes Maria home. I am fearful of a power failure in our lives.

She is now eighty-seven years old and still running the race. What is her secret? It is her intimacy with the Lord, no doubt about it. She lives to pray and to love her Lord and others. Our lives will never be the same because God brought Maria across our path when we most needed her.

Peter Deyneka, a Russian immigrant of many years ago, stayed in our home when I was a teenager. I remember his phrase, "Much prayer—much power; little prayer—little power." Maria understood it. I am beginning to understand it. Prayer has been my Achilles heel. Yet prayer is our lifeline. It is our oxygen. Trying to live without prayer is like trying to live without oxygen. It cannot be done.

I felt like I was at the twentieth mile of my marathon, the time when runners "hit the wall." I am not speaking from experience. I have never run in a marathon. You do remember why. I liked running fast but not far. I was at the wall. My spiritual legs were crying out, "Enough already!" My spiritual lungs were depleted. My mind was playing games with me. It kept telling me that I could not go on. The race was over for me. I was running up my last hill. And then when I came up over the hill, there was little Maria, like an oasis in my spiritual desert, offering me a cup of water, a spiritual nutrition bar, and some hearty words of encouragement. "You can do it, because you have me praying for you."

As you go about your daily life, and when you get discouraged by your circumstances, think of Maria. She lives to pray, and she wants to live as long as she can so she can pray for others. She knows the secret to victorious living. "Rejoice always! Pray without ceasing and in everything give thanks" (I Thessalonians 5:16–18, NKJV). Rejoice always! Pray always! Give thanks always! That's Maria. I am glad that you had a chance to meet her. Thanks, Maria, for allowing God to use you in our lives.

Oh, dear God, they fell asleep. What
more need Scripture say?
These, his very closest friends, were
asked to "watch and pray."

As wretched clouds of death and
doom their ugly shadows cast,
The next great act of God's great love
would yet now come to pass.

But, these, his loved ones, fell asleep,
devoid of spiritual power.

They heard the Master whisper, "Could
you not watch one hour?"

But do we have a stone to throw?
What have we to say?
Would we, in twilight's garden scene,
been more alert than they?
Do not, like Peter, James and
John we often fail to see
The depth of Jesus' call to prayer?
Oh, God, how can that be?

Dear Jesus, as we, by your side,
walk from day to day,
This one cry—we plead with thee:
"Teach us how to pray!"[2]

CHAPTER TWO

WHO ARE YOU, REALLY?

ROMANS 6:1–14

Who are you, really? If asked that question right now, how would you answer it? You might respond, "I am Mark the mechanic," or "Mike the medical doctor," or "Nancy the nurse," or "Connie the cook," or "Pat the pastor," or "Pete the plumber."

Many of us do not really understand who we are in Christ. An older couple, who were empty nesters, had a parrot. The man never liked the parrot. It only said three words: "Who is it?" All day long it would keep repeating those same three words. He was hopeful that someday the cage door would be left opened, the parrot would get out, and the cat would dispose of it quickly, with no remains.

One day, they needed to have a plumber come for some repair work. In the meantime, the man had to run to the hardware store, and his wife had a hair appointment. She wanted him to return in time to open the door for the plumber. He assured her that he would only be gone for a few minutes.

You guessed it; while he was gone, the plumber showed up. He was an old gentleman in the twilight years of his plumbing career. His heart was in a weakened condition. He brought his tools up on the porch, set them down, and proceeded to knock on the door. He heard this high-pitched, squeaky voice respond, "Who is it?" He replied rather loudly, "It's the plumber!" He waited for a moment, and no one responded, so he knocked rather vigorously one more time. That same shrill voice was heard coming from inside: "Who is it?" He shouted this time, "It's the plumber!" Again he waited for a half minute or so before he banged on the door a third time, loud enough for the neighbors to hear. Again this loud, shrill, high-pitched voice responded from inside, "Who is it?" The man screamed as loudly as he could, "It's the plumber!" At this point, the old man had a heart attack and crumpled up in a pile in front of the door.

The man of the house returned a moment later and ran up on the porch, trying to ascertain what needed to be done. At the same time, his wife pulled up in the driveway, leapt from her car, and ran up the steps to the porch screaming at the top of her lungs, "Who is it?"

From inside came this screeching but tiny voice, "It's the plumber."

WHO ARE YOU?

So, I ask you again, who are you, really? Knowing who

you are and what is available to you is essential if you are to run a good race and finish strong.

In understanding who you are, it is also imperative that you know whose you are. The great literary writer and evangelical thinker G.K. Chesterton was reportedly one day standing on a London street corner when he was approached by a newspaper reporter. He said to Dr. Chesterton, "Sir, I understand that you recently became a Christian. May I ask you one question?"

"Certainly," replied this great writer.

"If the risen Christ suddenly appeared at this very moment and stood behind you, what would you do?"

Chesterton looked directly into the eyes of the reporter and said, "He is."[3]

Living in the present, fully aware of His presence, is essential for runners who wish to finish their race. Jesus is present. He is watching. He is cheering us on. He is for us. Nobody wants to see us finish the race well more than Him.

But we get so caught up with our present problems that we forget He is there, present in our everyday experiences. He promised to never leave us nor forsake us. Matthew 28:20 reads, "And lo, I am with you always, even to the end of the age" (NKJV). That is not just a promise, but also a statement of fact.

The writer of Hebrews was writing to Jewish fellow believers who were being heavily persecuted for their faith. They had even lost everything in the way of material possessions according to Hebrews 10:34. But in Hebrews 13:5 we read, "Let your conduct be without covetousness; be content with such things as you have. For He Himself has said, 'I will never leave you nor forsake you'" (NKJV). In the Greek, it is a double negative meaning "I will never, never leave you." It is an impossibility that He would ever leave or abandon us.

The Message paraphrases the verse this way: "Don't be obsessed with getting more material things. Be relaxed with what you have. Since God assured us, 'I'll never let you down, never walk off and leave you,' we can boldly quote, God is there, ready to help; I'm fearless no matter what. Who or what can get to me?" (Hebrews 13:5–6).

OUR NEW IDENTITY IS IN HIM

His presence and person give us our identity. We call it ID (identification). You can hardly transact any business or board a commercial airliner or even traverse our highways without eventually needing your ID.

A country boy named Bubba was driving rather erratically through downtown Houston when he was pulled over by a city policeman. The policeman got out of his car, walked up to the window, and asked the red-neck, "You got any ID?"

Bubba responded, "'Bout what?"

What is our ID? God has Christ written all over us. We have His image stamped upon us. We are His by way of the new birth.

No section of Scripture better addresses our new identity than Romans 5 and 6. In Romans 1–3, Paul is writing to conclude that all are guilty of sin. There is not one person righteous in the eyes of God (Romans 3:10). "For all have sinned and come short of the glory of God" (Romans 3:23, NKJV). Then in Romans 3:24 and following, he shows how the righteousness of God is revealed apart from works or apart from the law. The righteousness comes to us through Jesus Christ. Abraham and David were both the recipients of this undeserved righteousness solely by their faith, as explained in chapter four.

Now, once we have received this righteousness by faith alone, we become the recipients of everything that God wants to give us because we are now His children. We have peace with God (5:1) and access to God (5:2). In verses 3–5, we can even rejoice in the most difficult trials in life because we are now His children, and there is no evil that can harm us apart from His sovereign will. We can even take comfort in knowing that He makes everything work together for good to those who love Him (8:28).

But right here in the midst of all of these wonderful benefits we have as His children, we find this section regarding our new identity. We were all born as descendants of the old Adam, the first Adam, and we inherited his sin nature. This becomes evident the moment we exit our mothers' wombs. We are self-centered, totally focused upon our own needs, with little thought about how our selfishness impacts and inconveniences the people around us who love us most. Unfortunately, we tend to live the rest of life the same way, apart from His indwelling life and presence.

Psalm 51:6 in the Amplified version reads, "Behold, I was brought forth in (a state of) iniquity; my mother was sinful who conceived me (and I, too, am sinful)."

In our text in Romans, we read, "Therefore, just as through one man sin entered the world, and death through sin, and thus death spread to all men, because all sinned" (Romans 5:12, NKJV).

I have often stated at funerals that this is the only answer as to why we die. Science has no satisfying answer. We die because of our sin nature. It was handed down to us from Adam. In Adam we sin and die. But the incredibly good news to nullify this is that in Christ we are all made righteous and alive. That is the bottom line of Romans 5:12–21. The contrast between the two Adams, the first and the last, could not be more stark and vivid.

OUR NEW IDENTITY COMES FROM OUR FAITH IN HIM

So now, through faith in Christ, I have a whole new identity. I am in a new family. I have a new Father. He is forever, and I am now in a forever family. I was physically born into a family that was kind of like the old TV families Ozzie and Harriet and Leave it to Beaver. These were the "stable" families back in the 1950s that stayed together and played together. As a child, I thought that my dad, mom, two brothers, and sister would be around forever. That was my sole identity. But now, my dad and mom are both gone, and my older brother is gone. I am now the oldest surviving member of my family, and I might add that my grandchildren already think that I am among the ancients. Our earthly family is very transitory, but our heavenly family is forever.

In Romans 6, Paul wants us to understand this new position and identity. As I have said before, unless you understand whose you are and who you are, you will probably never accomplish all of what God wants to do through you, and you will be likely to stumble and fall and quit the race before you ever see the finish line.

A parallel Scripture to this one is found in Ephesians 2. In the first three verses, Paul speaks of how we are dead, as it were, in our trespasses and sins. We were sucked into walking according to the wisdom of this present world. We were caught up in the fashions, fads, values, and futility of this culture. We were controlled by our own lusts and desires. We were under God's wrath and headed for a collision with God's final wrath. Fortunately, that is not the end of the story.

I am intrigued by the number of times the phrase "but God" occurs in Scripture. Here is one of them:

> But God, who is rich in mercy because of His great love with which He loved us, even when we were dead in trespasses, made us alive together with Christ (by grace you have been saved), and raised us up together and made us sit together in the heavenly places in Christ Jesus, that in the ages to come He might show the exceeding riches of His grace in His kindness toward us in Christ Jesus.
>
> Ephesians 2:4–7 (NKJV)

This is who we are, and this is where we are. Paul writes this in Colossians:

> If [better "since"] then you are raised with Christ, seek those things which are above, where Christ is, sitting at the right hand of God. Set your mind on things above, not on things on the earth. For you

died and your life is hidden with Christ in God.
When Christ who is our life appears, then you also
will appear with Him in glory.

Colossians 3:1–4 (NKJV)

The question then becomes one of appropriation.
Why do we not live more like those who are so positioned before him?

We were in Uganda in the summer of '06 for a large
pastors' wives conference, teaming up with evangelist
Sammy Tippit and his wife, Tex, who have been greatly
used of God throughout the Third World and beyond.
During the conference, we had an afternoon free to tour
the Rafiki homes for orphans not far from Kampala.

We were taken by car to a local church. There we
were asked to ride in an SUV with a young, attractive
African woman and her equally attractive female friend.
The driver wore military fatigues and had a machine
gun by his side. The man who climbed in behind us was
dressed the same way, with the same kind of weapon in
his hands. At first, I thought that they were there for
our protection, which was a rather vain thought. But
before long, we discovered through the young woman
who sat next to us, and was hesitant to tell us, that her
friend in the front seat was the daughter-in-law of the
president of Uganda. We had an interesting visit for
several hours, talking about everything from family, to

politics (including the war in Iraq), to spiritual matters. You name it, and we pretty much had the freedom to discuss it. It was a delightful time. Her family attends the church of a young man who spent many years in the states. He was discipled and educated here in San Antonio though Wayside Chapel and our dear friend and African American pastor, Rander Draper, at Maranatha Bible Church, on the northeast side of San Antonio. He and his lovely wife, Darlene, even had this young man living with them for a period of time. We never know how God is going to use us and how far and wide our influence might reach.

This young lady in the front seat was different. She lived with confidence. She held her head high. She had what seemed like an endless smile on her face. She stood out from the rest of the African women whom we met. There was something in her demeanor that set her apart from others. What was the reason for it? She knew who she was, the daughter-in-law of the president of Uganda. She might well be the next first lady of Uganda.

We too have been raised up and made to sit together with Christ in heavenly places. We are "children of God, and if children, then heirs—heirs of God and joint heirs with Christ, if indeed we suffer with Him that we may also be glorified together" (Romans 8:16–17, NKJV). It just doesn't get any better than that.

GETTING BEYOND BEING PARDONED

One author pictures a king who decrees that a pardon would be extended to all prostitutes. Would that be good news for you if you were a prostitute? Of course it would. You wouldn't have to worry anymore about avoiding the law, being arrested, or having a criminal record. The pardon would definitely be good news to you. But realistically, it wouldn't necessarily give you the motivation to change your lifestyle.

Now suppose that in addition to extending the pardon, the king were to come to you personally and ask you to become his wife. Would that give you a reason to change the way you live? Absolutely! Who wouldn't trade the life of a prostitute for that of a queen? Gaining a new identity as the king's wife would be your motivation to abandon prostitution.[4]

So many of us only thank God for the pardon extended. We are saved by grace, and we sing His praises because we are bound for heaven. Unfortunately, we never quite get to the point of living up to this new identity as kings and priests to God, and joint-heirs with Christ. Where is the power? I believe that the power comes from understanding who we are. Now let us look a little closer at the text here in Romans 6, which is so critical to our understanding.

THREE KEY WORDS IN ROMANS 6

Three words summarize the first fourteen verses of chapter 6. The first word is the word "know." It comes to us in verse 3 and again in verse 6. Paul puts it in the form of a question. I will state it as a fact. We must know that we were baptized into Christ. When He died, we died; when He was buried, we were buried; when He was raised to new life, we were raised to new life.

Without arguing the case, I do not believe that I am walking on thin ice when I make the statement that baptism in this passage is not referring to water baptism. I agree with the John MacArthur Study Bible notes on this passage. He writes,

This does not refer to water baptism. Paul is actually using the word "baptized" in a metaphorical sense, as we might in saying someone was immersed in his work, or underwent his baptism of fire when experiencing some trouble. All Christians have, by placing saving faith in Him, been spiritually immersed into the person of Christ, that is, united and identified with Him.[5]

The word "know" here is experiential in nature. He wants us to come to know and experience what really is the truth about us. We were taken out of Adam and placed into Christ. We have a whole new identity.

Marriage is a great illustration of this truth. Connie and I were married on July 1, 1962. At the moment her uncle, a pastor, pronounced us husband and wife, according to the laws of the state of Ohio, we were legally married. This was how the authorities now saw us, as husband and wife. Everything which I had, which was virtually nothing at the time, was now hers and vice versa. But did we make the adjustment into this new identity all at once? Not at all! I had lived as a single boy, spending much time on the farms. I had a lot to learn when it came to keeping clothes and everything in the house neat and orderly. I had to learn to squeeze the toothpaste from the end, not the middle and upwards. I had never even considered such things before, but she had. She had certain expectations of me. I was making progress. Likewise, there were certain things that she did which required some changing. One big change concerned her last name. It was no longer Hyde, but Troxel. Despite a few bank checks and introductions using her former last name, she accepted this new identity rather well.

We probably all know of someone or have seen

movies about someone who, for one reason or another, had to undergo a whole identity change. They changed their names, their social security numbers, and every other identifying factor that would leave any clue as to their whereabouts. Some end up in a witness protection program. They have a whole new identity. God delivered us from the power of darkness and conveyed us into the Kingdom of the Son of his love, and the good news is that the prince of the power of darkness cannot get his hands on us ever again. He has no power over us.

In the old hymn, "O for a Thousand Tongues to Sing," Charles Wesley expresses it well: "He breaks the power of cancelled sin. He sets the prisoner free. Tis music to the sinner's ears and life and health and peace."

In Romans 6:6, that old man that I once was no longer exists. The Amplified version brings this out best: "We know that our old (unrenewed) self was nailed to the cross with Him in order that our body, (which is the instrument) of sin, might be made ineffective and inactive for evil, that we might no longer be the slaves of sin."

I think of one of the scenes in the movie What About Bob. Bob, after being strapped to explosives by the psychiatrist, unties himself, jumps to his feet, and yells, "Free! I'm free!" thinking that he was free of all his emotional dysfunctions. But of course he wasn't. He could shout it, but he wasn't experiencing it. What was his problem? Why are we not experiencing this kind of victory over our own sin?

—

That brings us to the second word in verse 11. It is the word "reckon" in the NKJV. Some translations use the word "consider." We use this word rather loosely in conversation today. My dad used it this way. Often when he was asked if he would like to do something or go somewhere, he would respond with the words "I reckon." It didn't sound like a rousing affirmation. I always, with amusement, remember my dad on the day of his second wedding, nine years after my mother died. It was 1972. He brought his bride-to-be south to San Antonio, where I would have the privilege of uniting them in marriage. Our family and a few family members from out of state were there. It was a simple ceremony in what was then our church parsonage. I made it to the point in the ceremony where I asked my dad, "Do you take this woman to be your lawfully wedded wife?" You can see it coming. He responded, "I reckon." I looked him in the eye. This was one time that the son trumped the father. I said "Dad, that isn't good enough. Let me ask you again, 'Do you take this woman to be your lawfully wedded wife?'" He said, "I do." I do not recommend responding with "I reckon" as a way of scoring points with your new wife. I am not sure that she ever fully recovered from the trauma of that moment. Both have gone on to be with the Lord.

In reality, Dad was not too far from the truth, though he did not know it. The word "reckon" is close in meaning to the word "reconcile." When two people are reconciled, it means that they have been brought into agreement with one another.

The Greek word was a banker's term. Each month we get a statement from the bank that tells us how much we deposited, how much we withdrew, and any fees or charges, and then it finally gives us the balance. I don't know about you, but there have been many times over the years that what I showed in my checkbook and what the bank stated I had in the account did not match. In fact, there have been a few times when we weren't even "in the same zip code." Every time, barring none, it was my problem. I failed to register or subtract, or add a check. You know the routine. So I must reconcile my checkbook with the bank statement. The bank is fallible and makes mistakes, though they are seldom.

But God is infallible. God cannot lie (Titus 1:2). So if He says that I died with Christ and I was buried with Christ and I was raised again with Christ and now have new life, then I must simply reckon my account with His. I am dead. I am not the man that I once was. I now have new life that has been given to me. As we begin to count on the twin truth that we are dead to sin but alive unto God in union with Christ our Lord, our position becomes more and more an experiential reality. We don't have to give in to sin any longer. It is a present imperative verb meaning to always be reckoning yourselves to be dead indeed to sin, but alive to God in Christ Jesus our Lord. Then we can know in experience what Paul meant when he said, "For to me to live is Christ and to die is gain" (Philippians 1:21, NKJV).

> I have been crucified with Christ—(in Him) I have shared His crucifixion; it is no longer I who live, but Christ, the Messiah, lives in me; and the life I now live in the body I live by faith—by adherence to and reliance on and complete trust in the Son of God, who loved me and gave Himself up for me.
>
> Galatians 2:20 (AMP)

I have, over the years, struggled with anxiety attacks, almost always in the middle of the night. Worry is wasted energy. My only hope is in allowing Christ to take over my mind and body and live in me. When you are wronged, you can either seek vengeance or allow Christ to live in you. When your spouse offends or hurts you, you can either strike back or allow Christ to control you. When immoral thoughts bombard your mind, you can either entertain them or turn your thoughts heavenward. When thoughts of fear paralyze, you can allow them to immobilize your or you can scare them away with the remembrance that He is with you always. In other words, you have two choices: one is responding as the natural man in the flesh, and the other is responding as a spiritual man in the Spirit.

—

Now that brings us to the third and final word in the text. The word is "present" in verses 13 and 14:

> And do not present your members as instruments [weapons] of unrighteousness to sin, but present yourselves to God as being alive from the dead, and your members as instruments [weapons] of righteousness to God. For sin shall not have dominion over you, for you are not under law, but under grace.
>
> Romans 6:13–14 (NKJV)

The word "present" is the same word that is used in Romans 12:1:

> I appeal to you therefore, brethren, and beg of you in view of all the mercies of God, to make a decisive dedication of your bodies—presenting all your members and faculties—as a living sacrifice, holy (devoted, consecrated) and well pleasing to God, which is your reasonable (rational, intelligent) service and spiritual worship.
>
> Romans 12:1 (AMP)

In the Greek, it is a once and for all presenting of your body and its members to God. As in marriage, it is a once and for all giving of yourself to your spouse. But then there is the daily, even moment by moment presentation to our loved one as well.

Present has the meaning of placing before, or putting yourself at one's disposal. It was used in a military sense. It could also be used of tools given to the slave for daily use. Every morning the slave would present himself and his tools to his master for his use. Each morning the soldier rises and readies himself to present himself and his weaponry to his commanding officer. Tools and weapons were not given to be used for selfish purposes and personal gratification.

If I understand this rightly, then each morning when I get up I need to present every part of my body to Him. I might pray, "These eyes belong to You, Lord Jesus. Let them only look at the things that are pleasing to You. These hands belong to You, Lord Jesus. Let them only do Your work and nothing else today. These feet, they too belong to You, Lord Jesus. Let them take me no place today where You do not feel comfortable and at home."

A ONCE AND FOR ALL DAILY PRESENTATION TO HIM

This once and for all gift, along with the daily presentation of our entire minds and bodies to Him, constitutes part of the secret of overcoming sin.

There is another factor best illustrated by the following story from an unknown source. A pilot was flying his small plane one day when he heard a noise that he recognized as the gnawing of a rat. Wondering what its sharp teeth were cutting through, he suddenly realized with horror that it might be a wire critical to the airplane's operation. Then he remembered that rodents can't survive at high altitudes. Immediately he put his oxygen mask on and began climbing from 4,000 feet to 6,000, then 8,000 and 10,000 feet, finally arriving at 12,000 feet. Soon the gnawing was less and less until it eventually ceased altogether and when he landed he found the rat—dead.

This story illustrates how we must deal with sin. We must fly higher. This is the theme of Paul in Romans 6–8: how to fly higher.

Galatians 5:16 reads, "Walk in the Spirit and you shall not fulfill the lust of the flesh" (NKJV).

Fly higher!

"But put on the Lord Jesus Christ and make no provision for the flesh, to fulfill its lusts" (Romans 13:14, NKJV).

Fly higher and finish well. Pursue Christ until you cross that finish line.

My spirit, soul and body, Jesus I give to thee,
A consecrated offering, thine evermore to be.

O Jesus, mighty Savior, I trust in thy great name;
I look for thy salvation, thy promise now I claim.

Now, Lord, I yield my members, from sin's dominion free,
For warfare and for triumph, as weapons unto thee.

Oh, blissful self-surrender, to live, my Lord, by thee!
Now, Son of God, my Savior, live out thy life in me.

I'm thine, O blessed Jesus! Washed
in thy precious blood,
Sealed by thy Holy Spirit, a sacrifice to God.[6]

CHAPTER THREE
MEET DAVID ALLEN—A MAN OF THE WORD

Meet Pastor David Allen. Pastor Allen was pastor of Calvary Baptist Church in Hazel Park, a northern suburb of Detroit, Michigan. Many of the college students from Detroit Bible College, later called William Tyndale College, attended there. I was busy trying to carry a full-time load at that college, work a full-time job, and be a husband to Connie and a father to our newborn daughter, Shelli. I didn't know the meaning of the word "stress" at that time, and I'm not sure that it was even part of my vocabulary. But that is what it was.

I had very little time to sleep at night. This was during the booming years of the car manufacturers in Detroit. It was 1964. I was working at Chrysler, operating a forklift, for forty hours a week. Then they increased our overtime to forty-four hours a week, and eventually it ended up at fifty-four hours per week. They could not keep up with the demand for cars. On top of that, I was carrying a full load at the college: first fifteen hours, but then I dropped a three-hour course and even considered dropping out of school altogether.

A MAN OF THE WORD

Our one really bright spot in the week was going to hear this gifted expositor of the Scriptures speak. The Word was like a salve, soothing my wounded psyche each Sunday. I was amazed at his memory. He could stand for forty-five minutes, speaking on a given topic without notes, and quote verbatim sixty or so various passages of Scripture, giving it word for word, book, chapter, and verse, seldom misquoting or getting any part of it wrong. I know because I would try to catch his mistakes.

Pastor Allen could speak on the deity of Christ. He would give us sixty different quotes from Old and New Testaments on the deity of Christ. Each Sunday, we would leave astounded at the authority of the Word of God. Anyone who had an argument with him really had an argument with God's Word.

He also had a great sense of humor. I remember hearing him preach on the book of Revelation. One Sunday he came to chapter 20 and the Great White Throne Judgment where John writes, "And I saw the dead, small and great, standing before God, and books were opened. And another book was opened, which is the Book of Life. And the dead were judged according to their works, by the things which were written in the books." His comments went something like this: "This judgment is not to determine where they are going. These are all going to hell. This is to see where in hell they go; North hell, South hell, East hell or West hell. South hell is probably hotter than North hell. It will be worse for some than others."

HOW THE WORD WAS IMPACTING ME

God was building into my life two things during that year. First, He was confirming in me the absolute trustworthiness of His Word. If you were around and remember the turbulent '60s, you will recall that liberalism and higher criticism were making great inroads into our academic institutions. This was the beginning of the "God is dead" movement in Western culture. I had just assumed God to be alive and for His Word to be true. I was raised in a very conservative Bible-believing church. Remember the old bumper sticker, "God said it. I believe it. That settles it"? There was one glaring problem with that sticker. God's Word is true whether I believe it or not. But up to that time I had no reason to question the Word. Any concerns that I might have had seemed to dissipate as we sat under Pastor Allen's teaching week after week, experiencing first-hand the power and authority of the Word of God.

I mentioned two things that God was doing in me. The second thing was this: If I wanted to be used as

David Allen and speak with the same authority as he, then I too must memorize and meditate on the Word of God. I had heard that he rose at 4:00 a.m. each morning and reviewed 400 verses of Scripture. Whether or not that was true, it was obvious that he was mastering the Word and allowing the Word to master him.

Back in the mid-1980s, now as an older man, I invited him to come to Wayside and speak for a weekend of meetings. He was still mentally sharp and effective. Again, we experienced that same sense of being influenced by the power of the Word. He ran well and the good news is that he finished well. I had a chance to thank him for the difference his example had made in my life. David Allen was one who encouraged me in the beginning of my marathon to be strong in the Word.

You see, I began to carry a little New Testament containing the Psalms and Proverbs with me everywhere I went. We had ten-minute coffee breaks every two hours at Chrysler. I would get off in a corner somewhere and work on memorizing key verses. Then I began to memorize chapters and finally I turned to memorizing whole books.

Oh, I must tell you that I haven't hidden as much of the Word in my life as David Allen did, but I can tell you that he challenged me to make it a lifelong discipline, and what I have put there has been quite useful to me over the years and has kept me in the race.

God's Word in my heart and memory has done many wonderful things for me. It has kept my mind active (saying "sharp" might be questionable to my friends who know me well). I am amazed at how I can be preaching in large and small venues and the Word will come to me, sometimes passages which I haven't reviewed or read in quite some time. I believe that this is the ministry of the Holy Spirit.

Second, I cannot tell you how much sin that this practice might have kept me from over the years. I discovered decades ago that I could not be memorizing and meditating on the Word and sinning with my mind at the same time. It is virtually impossible. Most sin begins with too much free time and having the mind disengaged. The enemy loves to fill an empty mind. Remember the saying "an idle mind is the devil's workshop?"

Third, there have been so many times over the years when the enemy has come at me like a flood, with one of his "flaming missiles" (Ephesians 6:16). These flaming missiles are designed to hit their target and render it inoperable. It might be a fleeting (hopefully that's all) thought involving another woman. Most men struggle with this. She is attractive. She is sexy. She is desirable.

If you have no other restraints there to hold you back, what is to keep you, like David of old, from taking her to yourself?

God's Word has been like a hammer in my life (Jeremiah 23:29), reminding me of where the sin of adultery eventually leads one. Passages like Proverbs 5, 6, 7, and 9 remind us of the high cost of this kind of sin. King David's example is a reminder. That relationship can even lead to death and often does. Proverbs 9:17–18 reminds us sin is costly: "Stolen water is sweet, and bread eaten in secret is pleasant. But he does not know that the dead are there, and that her guests are in the depths of sheol [the grave]" (NKJV). "Her house is the way to sheol, descending to the chambers of death" (Proverbs 7:27, NKJV). Steve Farrar has written,

> In nautical history, there are three inescapable consequences to being shipwrecked that are true whether it's inland on the Mississippi or out on the open sea: shipwrecks can take you farther than you wanted to go; shipwrecks can keep you longer than you wanted to stay; and shipwrecks can cost you more than you wanted to pay.[7]

I have tweaked that just a bit for remembrance purposes: "sin will take you further then you ever wanted to stray, keep you longer then you ever wanted to stay, and cost you more then you ever wanted to pay." I saw this happen with my older brother. The other woman did cost him his life. He had been so badly deceived by the enemy that he chose to end his life at age forty-eight.

A church sign read, "Forbidden fruit creates many jams."[8]

As a pastor, even if your life is spared, your ministry and influence are greatly diminished.

Jesus used the Word when He encountered the devil in the wilderness. In Matthew 4, as the devil tempted him to compromise and listen to him, Jesus could say, "It is written."

How interesting that this incident would be right up front at the very beginning of His ministry. Of course He had to be tested before He began. But I believe that He was also showing us that we cannot survive the enemy's onslaught without the Word. Having the Word written in our hearts will, in our moments of greatest temptation, sustain us.

Every Scripture is God-breathed—given by His inspiration—and profitable for instruction, for reproof and conviction of sin, for correction of error and discipline in obedience, and for training in righteousness (that is, in holy living, in conformity to God's will in thought, purpose and action), so that the man of God may be complete and proficient, well-fitted and thoroughly equipped for every good work.

II Corinthians 3:16–17 (AMP)

DAILY MEMORIZATION AND MEDITATION

Sometimes we mistakenly think that it is the college or seminary that prepares us for ministry. I am not opposed to further studies and I even recommend them. But many pastors in the developing countries may have no opportunity to have further training. It is really the Word of God that gives us our authority. Formal study helps us in getting a better grasp on the Word and gives us tools to do so. But I believe that the man who daily meditates in the Word and memorizes it is promised to be fruitful. Psalm 1:1–3 promises us that.

The Word has corrected my thinking and brought distortions back into clear focus hundreds of times. The Word has also comforted me in countless ways. One of the first whole books I had memorized was the little book of Philippians. I was then in my second year of seminary. It was a disastrous year health-wise. It began with our older daughter Shelli, then five, developing juvenile diabetes, and continued with my wife having to have one of her kidneys removed—probably a congenital problem—and culminated with me developing Addison's disease, which the doctors acknowledge that I will have the rest of my life.

Trying to stay in seminary, pastor a church, and work part-time was not easy. Then we were not prepared to have a daughter with this kind of a physical problem. We were in our mid-twenties. What did the future hold for her and for us? Why us, God? She was hospitalized fifty miles away in Akron Children's Hospital. I would pick up our youngest daughter, Kelli, who was only four at the time, from her grandma's and head for home. Sleep was hard to come by. My mind was racing with fear as I looked to the future. Then one night in the darkness, this passage in Philippians 4:4 came to light. I was to rejoice, give thanks, not be anxious, and let the peace of God guard my heart and mind (4:7).

And God's peace (shall be yours, that tranquil state of a soul assured of its salvation through Christ, and so fearing nothing from God and content with its earthly lot of whatever sort that is, that peace) which transcends all understanding, shall garrison and mount guard over your hearts and minds in Christ Jesus.

Philippians 4:7 (AMP)

I often challenge pastors, who have little or no opportunity to go for further biblical training, to memorize the Word. There are 7,959 verses in the New Testament. If you memorize one verse per day, you can memorize the whole New Testament in twenty-two years, if two verses per day, in eleven years, and if three verses per day, you could do it all in seven years. If we have God's Word in our mind, He can put the right words in our mouths.

This may seem a bit overwhelming, but we each need to start somewhere. I started with individual verses, then paragraphs, then chapters, and finally whole books. Begin with a book like Philippians, the epistle of joy. In chapter one Christ is our life, in chapter two our mind, in chapter three our goal, and in chapter four our strength. This practice of memorizing could change your life and keep you running your race.

Thank you, David Allen, for motivating me to equip myself with the Sword of the Spirit, which is the Word of God (Ephesians 6:17). You challenged me early in my run and gave me courage from the Word to both start and stay in the race.

"His Word in My Life"

His Word in my life is my guide book
to keep me from straying away.
His word in my life is my soul food
that I need to partake of each day.

His Word in my life will convict me,
demanding I alter direction.
His Word in my life will impact me, bringing much needed correction.

His Word in my life keeps me running, not falling out of the race.
His Word in my life will sustain me
until we are face–to-face.

Pastor Steve

CHAPTER FOUR
LOOKING UNTO JESUS
HEBREWS 11, 12

One of the portions of Scripture that has kept me running has been the book of Hebrews. A friend of mine, Dr. Dave Player, and I memorized this book back in the mid-1980s. It has been a source of strength to me ever since.

The book was written to encourage Jewish believers in their faith. They were in danger of going back to Judaism and legalism. The writer of Hebrews writes of the supremacy and sufficiency of Christ in every area of life. He is greater than anything that their old way of life and tradition had to offer them. The same is true for each one of us. When we are in danger of wavering in our faith, we need to consume a good dose of the book of Hebrews.

THOSE WHO LIVED BY FAITH BEFORE US

They had given up everything and even lost everything of material value according to chapter 10. Life was difficult. They were being persecuted for their faith in Christ, just as some of you reading this chapter are experiencing at this very time. But in chapter 11 the writer encourages his readers to a life of faith. Without faith, it is impossible to please God (11:6). He then gives examples of the lives of the great characters of the Old Testament, men and women who walked by faith and kept their eyes focused on the Eternal One.

Moses was a great example.

> By faith Moses, when he became of age, refused to be called the son of Pharaoh's daughter, choosing rather to suffer affliction with the people of God than to enjoy the passing pleasures of sin, esteeming the reproach of Christ greater riches than the treasures in Egypt; for he looked to the reward. By faith he forsook Egypt, not fearing the wrath of the king; for he endured as seeing Him who is invisible.
>
> Hebrews 11:24–26 (NKJV)

The NLT renders the last part of verse 27, "He kept his eyes on the One who is invisible." This expression was used of an artist or sculptor keeping his eyes focused on what he is reproducing. We have all seen these artists at work in tourist areas, intently fixed on the form and face of the object that they are reproducing. This is the idea in this passage.

What each of these great saints had in common was their faith in the Unseen Ruler of the universe.

IT IS NOT THE AMOUNT BUT THE OBJECT OF OUR FAITH

These Old Testament saints were resting in Him because the issue is never the amount of one's faith, but rather the object of that faith. Charles Price gives a great illustration of this from his own life. He tells of his first airplane ride from England to Zimbabwe, Africa. He found himself boarding a Boeing 707, which has rows of three seats on either side of the plane. He was in the middle seat. Next to the window was a very nervous, elderly woman whose knuckles were gripping the armrest tightly. This was her first time in an airplane. On the other side of him, in the seat next to the aisle, was a South African businessman. He had flown many times before. He showed little concern about the flight.

Price writes:

> Presently we started to move toward the end of the runway and prepare for take-off. As the engines opened up the woman next to me seemed to shrivel in fear. As the noise of the engines got louder she seemed to get smaller. Presently we began to move, and as we lifted off the ground her head was tucked into her lap, just waiting for something to go wrong. I was at the same time experiencing a combination of exhilaration on the one hand and fear on the other. The man on my right, in contrast to both of us, was completely relaxed and at ease. He just continued

to read his book. It was a sixteen-hour journey to Zimbabwe with three stops en-route. During that time the woman began to relax just a little, I relaxed much, much more, and the man on my right was completely relaxed as he ate, read, drank, or slept.[9]

His point was that each one had a different level of faith. But each had enough faith to get on the plane. Besides, they all arrived at the same time at the same destination. It was not the quality of the faith but the object of the faith that is all-important. Each of these Old Testament saints had different levels of faith, but in the same invisible, all-powerful God.

The writer of Hebrews goes from these saints, who made it into Faith's Hall of Fame chapter, to Christ Himself in chapter 12. Peterson's translation of these first three verses in chapter 12 is quite helpful:

Do you see what this means—all these pioneers who blazed the way, all these veterans cheering us on? It means we'd better get on with it. Strip down, start running—and never quit! No extra spiritual fat, no parasitic sins. Keep your eyes on Jesus, who both began and finished this race we're in. Study how he did it. Because he never lost sight of where he was headed—that exhilarating finish in and with God—he could put up with anything along the way: cross, shame, whatever. And now He's there, in the place of honor, right alongside God. When you find yourselves flagging in your faith, go over that story again, item by item, that long litany of hostility He plowed through. That will shoot adrenaline into your souls.

Hebrews 12:1–3 (MSG)

One of the classic stories in sports history tells of an athlete who ran the wrong way. Wrong Way Riegels is a familiar one. On New Year's Day, 1929, Georgia Tech played UCLA in the Rose Bowl. In that game, a young man named Roy Riegels recovered a fumble for UCLA. Picking up the loose ball, he lost his direction and ran sixty-five yards toward the wrong goal line. One of his teammates, Benny Lom, ran him down and tackled him just before he scored for the opposing team. Several plays later, the Bruins had to punt. Tech blocked the kick and scored a safety, demoralizing the UCLA team.

That strange play came in the first half. At halftime, the UCLA players filed off the field and into the dressing room. As others sat down on the benches and the floor, Riegels put a blanket around his shoulders, sat down in a corner, and put his face in his hands.

A football coach usually has a great deal to say to his team during halftime. That day, Coach Price was quiet. No doubt he was trying to decide what to do with Riegels. When the timekeeper came in and announced that there were three minutes before the second half would begin, Coach Price looked at the team and said, "Men, the same team that played the first half will start the second." The players got up and started out, all but Riegels. He didn't budge. The coach looked back and called to him. Riegels didn't move. Coach Price went over to where Riegels sat and said, "Roy, didn't you hear me? The same team that played the first half will start the second."

Roy Riegels looked up; his cheeks were wet with tears and he said, "Coach, I can't do it. I've ruined the university's reputation. I've ruined myself. I can't face that crowd out there." Coach Price reached out, put his hand on Riegels' shoulder, and said "Roy, get up and go on back. The game is only half over."

All one needs to do is give a cursory glance to the great saints mentioned in chapter 11 to show that many of them, including the greatest patriarch, Abraham, and the greatest Old Testament prophet of them all, Moses, did not have a good first half. Of course the Apostles did not have a good beginning either. At the cross, they all forsook him and fled. But as the old saying goes, it is not how well you do in the beginning of the race but how well you finish. We do not remember how runners start, but rather how they finish.

If you are reading these words and discouraged

about how well you are running, don't give up. Keep your eyes on the prize. Keep your eyes fixed on Jesus.

I remember shortly after my mother died in 1963 that I heard a message on this passage depicting this great crowd of witnesses in verse 1 as being in a coliseum or stadium, and they are watching intently as we are running the race and they are cheering us on. It seemed comforting to know that my mother was now watching me run my race. Comforting, that is, until I stumbled and fell along the way. And there have been many failures. I thought to myself, Mother cannot be enjoying herself in heaven too much right now. Is this really what the passage is teaching? Probably not! More likely he is picturing athletes in a foot race, running for the finish line and urged on by a crowd of spectators. He no doubt had in mind both witnesses and spectators. He may have had in mind a relay race where the baton is passed from one runner to another. Those who have completed their segment of the relay (i.e., the heroes of faith mentioned in chapter 11) stand to encourage their successors.

I don't think that this passage is teaching us that our loved ones in heaven are watching each move we make and seeing us stumble and even fall flat on our faces at times. That would be painful for them, and in the eternal state, there is no more pain (Revelation 21:4).

THESE A

What then were these sain.
bear witness that God's people
word "martyr" comes from the C
"witness." In Acts 14:22 we read tha
abas returned again to Lystra, Iconiu. ...och
of Pisidia, where they strengthened the be ...rs. They
encouraged them to continue in the faith, reminding
them that they must enter into the Kingdom of God
through many tribulations" (NLT). Each of the saints
mentioned in chapter 11 suffered in one way or another
because of their faith, and yet it was their faith that
kept them running right through the difficulties. Your
faith can do that for you just as well.

Second, they bear witness to the fact that after the
suffering comes the glory. This is a principle brought
out throughout scripture. First comes the suffering,
and then the glory. First is the hardship, and then
comes heaven. When Jesus revealed Himself to the two
disciples on the road to Emmaus on the day of His
resurrection, He referred to them as foolish ones and
slow of heart.

They were slow of heart to believe in all that the
prophets have spoken! Ought not the Christ to have
suffered these things and to enter into His glory?

ginning at Moses and all the prophets, He
xpounded (explained) to them in all the Scriptures
the things concerning Himself.

Luke 24:25–26 (NKJV)

Every runner must not only prepare physically, but
also mentally, to run. We all know of excellent athletes
who never made it to the top of their competition and
won the ultimate prize, not because of lack of physical
preparation, but rather a lack of mental preparedness.
It is customary in professional athletics today, when a
game is lost, for the losing athletes to confess that they
just weren't mentally prepared. Mental preparation is
the responsibility of both the coach and the players.
They weren't mentally prepared. They were distracted.

If you are going to run in a marathon, you must
mentally prepare yourself that it is going to be a long
and grueling race and then you begin to physically prepare for it. The mental preparation must come first,
and it must remain not only throughout the preparation, but also throughout the race.

The mind must win out over the body. This is what
Paul is saying in I Corinthians 9:24–27. He speaks of
buffeting his body. He is not referring to going to the "all
you can eat" places. He refers to bringing your body into
subjection. You run and run and run. You run in good
weather and in bad weather. Long distance runners will

sometimes run 100 miles or more per week preparing for that twenty-six-mile and 385-yard run. Some trace the beginning back to 490 b.c. A legendary Greek runner ran from Marathon, Greece, to Athens for the purpose of proclaiming the victory over the Persians. It was a popular race in New Testament times and could have been what the writer of Hebrews had in mind here.

THE PREPARATION FOR THE RACE

If we are going to run a great race and finish well, what must we do? We must strip down. In 12:1, we read, "Let us lay aside every weight and the sin which so easily ensnares us" (NKJV). The imagery is setting one free from that which would encumber us; weights and sins are different. We know of people today who are deliberately seeking to keep their lives simple so they can be free to respond in their giving and going where God calls. In fact, my wife and I are close friends with two couples, of whom all four mates are doctors, with various specialties, who have chosen to live simple lifestyles. They are involved in lucrative professions, yet they live very modestly and give very generously. They are in the race to win.

I love the story that Paul Harvey shared years ago about the Italian sailing team racing in the American Cup. The race that year was held in Australia. On one of their days off, the Italian team decided to rent a Jeep and go into the outback to enjoy the scenery and see if they could get a glimpse of a kangaroo or two. The team had been completely outfitted by the Italian designer Gucci. They wore Gucci jackets, carried Gucci bags, and wore Gucci watches.

As they were driving through the Outback, a kangaroo hopped in front of them. Unable to stop the Jeep in time, they hit the kangaroo, and it fell on the road in front of them—apparently dead. The team members all jumped out to take a look. Someone suggested, "Let's at least take a picture!"

The driver suggested, "Before we take the picture, I'll put my jacket on it so it looks like even kangaroos wear Gucci clothes!"

They put the jacket on the limp animal, and as they stepped back to take the picture the kangaroo suddenly revived and hopped into the brush—wearing the jacket. Unfortunately, the driver's keys and wallet and American Express card were in the jacket. One of these days, all of our material possessions will be gone just like that. Proverbs 23:4–5 reads, "Do not overwork to be rich: Because of your own understanding, cease. Will you set your eyes on that which is not? For riches certainly make themselves wings: They fly away like an eagle toward heaven" (NKJV).

I purposed years ago that I would never use the ministry to build great material wealth. And I can tell you that I have managed to definitely succeed at fulfilling that purpose.

We all know that there is nothing wrong with having material possessions as long as those material possessions do not have us. It is okay to possess earthly possessions if those earthly possessions do not possess us. But, as my dad used to say, "The more we have, the more we have to worry about." As a runner, all of that weight will keep you from running and finishing your race.

John Ruskin has written, "Every increased possession loads us with a new weariness."

Runners peal off all unnecessary clothes.

We are reminded of this every time we travel to a foreign country. Restrictions in airline travel have made it mandatory that we travel lightly. We have been without extra clothes for as long as six days. It was the same clothes day after day. We did not have to take the time to choose what we were going to wear that next day. It made life quite simple. We also remember another couple who traveled with us to Europe years ago. They took an extremely large suitcase. We took two small ones. The one large one was much more difficult to maneuver in trains and busses as well as planes. We all served time pushing and pulling that large suitcase around.

You might be a pastor of a congregation in a less affluent country. There is so much wisdom in the Sermon on the Mount portion in Matthew 6, where Jesus said that just as God takes care of the birds and the lilies of the field, so He is going to take care of you. Why? Because you are so much more valuable than each of them. In many ways you are far more blessed than those who are living in the midst of wealth. I think that Jesus would even say that you are blessed because of it. Wealth and material possessions can become a curse. In the parable of the sower in Luke 8:14, the good seed does not bear fruit among the thorns because these are "those who, when they have heard, go out and are choked with cares, riches, and pleasures of life, and bring no fruit to maturity" (NKJV).

> Now godliness with contentment is great gain. For we brought nothing into this world and it is certain that we can take nothing out. And having food and clothing, with these we shall be content. But those who desire to be rich fall into temptation and a snare, and into many foolish and harmful lusts which drown men in destruction and perdition.
>
> I Timothy 6:6–9 (NKJV)

The sins mentioned here that so easily ensnare us can be many things. Certainly, sex can be one of them. And a person's age is no guarantee of success in this area. Steve Farrar tells about a young pastor named John Bisagno who later became the senior pastor of the large First Baptist Church of Houston. When he was about to finish college, he was having dinner over at his fiancée's house one night. After dinner, he was talking with his future father-in-law, Dr. Paul Beck, out on the porch. Dr. Beck had been in ministry for years, and that was inevitably the subject toward which the conversation turned. "John, as you get ready to enter the ministry, I want to give you some advice," Dr. Beck told the younger man. "Stay true to Jesus! Make sure that you keep your heart close to Jesus every day. It's a long way from here to where you're going to go, and Satan is in no hurry to get you."[10]

We are never beyond his reach.

Or it can be the sin of anger or revenge or bitterness. We all struggle with envy when others appear to be more successful than we are.

Even disappointment and discouragement, which are caused by losing our focus, can be sins that ensnare and cause us to drop out of the race.

PERSEVERANCE IN THE RACE

We must start and continue running. The writer of Hebrews continues, "Let us run with patience [endurance] the race that is set before us" (Hebrews 12:1, NKJV). It is a race, a marathon, not a sprint. We must keep reminding ourselves of this truth. The Greek word for race is "agona." It gives us our English word "agonize." We all know what it means to agonize. We think of the agony of Christ in Gethsemane.

In the sporting world, I think of Lance Armstrong, who is known the world over for winning the Tour de France bicycle race seven years in a row. Racing through the mountains, when most men begin to falter, is where Lance appears to excel. He speaks of the agony, even to the point that he thinks that he is going to die. They average over twenty-five mph over the course of a day, uphill and downhill, wet roads, dry roads, day in and day out for nearly three weeks. I would imagine it is much more agonizing than a marathon. Lance can only do it by keeping his eyes on the yellow shirt and the trophy. Most would believe that even more important than his superior athletic conditioning is his mental toughness that kept him riding and winning.

Some of you are trying to race up some pretty steep mountains today. You have slowed almost to a halt. You are about to climb down off your bike and give it up.

Worse yet, you have stopped mentally. You might even be standing by the side of the road just watching others go by. Or maybe you are flat on your back, hardly aware that others are passing you by. Our world is filled with former runners and former racers. The agony did them in.

You have encountered an obstacle that has you sidelined. There is nothing that can keep you from finishing your race unless you allow it to. Even when your health is failing, you can still be used by God. It all depends on what we call mental toughness. Bill Bright, founder of Campus Crusade, recently went home to be with the Lord. Several years ago, he was diagnosed with pulmonary thrombosis. In a letter, just before his home-going, he said that his last two years had been his most productive: writing, editing, producing teaching videos, and co-founding a global network aimed at starting five million house churches, even though he has been on oxygen treatment most of the time.

Maybe you have gone through moral failure and you were misled by the devil into believing that you can never be used of God again. As devastating as the consequences can be, God has not given up on you. He wants to use you. If He were finished with you, He would have taken you home by now.

Jesus prayed, "I have glorified You on the earth; I

have finished the work which You have given Me to do. And now O Father, glorify Me together with Yourself, with the glory which I had with You before the world was" (John 17:4–5, NKJV).

The only reason God keeps us here is that He is not finished with us yet. So get up and keep running.

A wonderful allegory gives us great encouragement: Once upon a time, a young donkey asked his grandpa, "How do I grow up to be just like you?"

"Oh, that really is quite simple," Grandpa said. "All you have to do is shake it off and step up."

"What does that mean?" asked the young donkey.

Grandpa said, "Let me tell you a story. When I was just about your age, I was out walking one day and I wasn't paying much attention to where I was going and I fell into a deep, old, abandoned well. I started braying and braying. Finally an old farmer came by and heard my cry and saw me down in that deep well. I was scared to death. And then he left. I stayed in that well all night.

"The next morning he came back with a whole group of people, and they looked down at me. Some of them even laughed. Then the old farmer said, 'The well is abandoned and that donkey isn't worth saving, so let's get started.' And would you believe it—they started to bury me alive!

"Well, I panicked. I was going to be buried alive!

"After the first shovel full of dirt came down on me, I realized something. Every time dirt landed on my back, I could shake it off and step up. They kept shoveling, and I kept shaking it off and stepping up. This went on for some time. 'Shake it off and step up. Shake it off and step up.' I kept repeating it to myself for encouragement. I fought the panic by shaking it off and stepping up. And it wasn't long before I stepped out of the well, exhausted but triumphant.

"So, no matter how difficult the situation or no matter how bad things get, and no matter how much dirt gets dumped on you, just remember to shake it off and step up."[11]

Some of you are in a hole. Others are throwing dirt at you. Maybe you are throwing unnecessary dirt at yourself. If there has been true repentance, just shake it off, step up, and start running again.

OUR PROTOTYPE FOR THE RACE

Finally, we must keep our eyes on Jesus. We are to run "looking unto Jesus, the author and finisher of our faith, who for the joy that was set before Him endured the cross, despising the shame, and has sat down at the right hand of the throne of God" (Hebrews 12:2, NKJV).

If you look closely at me, you will discover flaws. I will fail you. If I look long enough at you, you will fail me. We both will be disappointed in one another. But He is the victorious pioneer or pathfinder or trailblazer of our faith. He is the One who takes the lead and furnished the supreme example of one who suffered, endured, and finished and in the process perfected or completed our salvation. He accomplished His mission. His cross was not a failure, but rather a mighty victory. The word "perfector" or "finisher" comes from the Greek word "teleios." It was the word that Jesus used when He cried out on the cross, "It is finished!"

In basketball, we have a word for someone who is able to take it to the basket and then finish with a score. We call him or her a "finisher." In all the effort, they do not allow themselves to come up empty-handed. Jesus completed what He came for. Even in the midst of all of the hostility, adversity, and opposition, He would not allow it to distract Him from His mission. The enemy threw every temptation in His arsenal at him in Matthew 4. But He was not about to allow the temptations to lead to sinning.

How did He withstand all of that temptation? How did He finish well? The bottom line is that He looked beyond the present suffering to the glory that awaited Him. The text refers to "the joy that was set before him." Because of that, He "endured the cross, despising the shame." The NLT renders it: "He was willing to die a shameful death on the cross because of the joy he knew would be his afterward" (Hebrews 12:2b).

Paul finished well because of this great example. He emulated his Savior. In II Corinthians 4, Paul speaks of living in constant danger of death, hunted down like a wild animal, crushed by his circumstance, at times even to the point of despair, yet very much mindful of the resurrection of Christ and all that His life means.

> That is why we never give up. Though our bodies are dying, our spirits are being renewed every day. For our present troubles are quite small and won't last very long. Yet they produce for us an immeasurable greater glory that will last forever! So we don't look at the troubles we can see right now; rather, we look forward to what we have not yet seen. For the troubles we see will soon be over, but the joys to come will last forever.
>
> II Corinthians 4:16–18 (NLT)

That ought to get you back into the running of the race. If it was good enough for Jesus and good enough for Paul, it is good enough for me and good enough for you.

John Fischer writes about a church in Old Greenwich, Connecticut, which has something highly unusual in it. It has a cross in it, not behind the platform or high up in the ceiling, but rather, mounted straight in front of the pulpit, not more than three feet from where the preacher stands. It is a sturdy wooden cross standing ten feet tall. It is set in concrete and bolted to the floor. It is never moved. While the pastor preaches, it is there. When the choir sings, it is there. When a bride and groom get married, it is there. When a baby is dedicated, it is somewhere near the cross. When a casket is wheeled in for a funeral, they have to deal with that cross.

It is a constant reminder that the pathway to glory is the pathway of suffering. Are you down, defeated, and discouraged? Look to that cross. Pastor, don't look at your numbers, look to the Cross. Don't look at others that appear to be more successful than you. Look to the Cross. Don't even look back at your sin. If repented of, it is all covered by that cross.

The old song by Helen H. Lemmel states it so well: "O soul, are you weary and troubled, no light in your darkness can see. There is light for a look at the Savior, a life more abundant and free. (Chorus) Turn your eyes upon Jesus. Look full in his wonderful face. And the things of earth will grow strangely dim, in the light of his glory and grace."

"Finish Well"

Are you looking down the road? Can
you see around the bend?
Will the final gun still find you
are running at the end?

Satan knows you've shed some weights;
he has seen you pick up speed;
He has also planted in your heart
seeds of anger, seeds of greed.

His great goal, as life goes on, isn't
what your past can tell.
What he longs to do, dear friend, is
see that you don't finish well!

His great goal, as life goes on, as
you're nearer heaven's call,
Is before the final gun, just to see you slip and fall.

His desire, and mark it well, is for
God on that great day,
Filled with grief, to have to cry,
"You became a castaway!"

May we rather, on that day, as the devil rots in hell,
Hear the Master gently say, "Child
of mine, you finished well!"[12]

CHAPTER FIVE

MEET RAY STEDMAN—A PASTOR TO PASTORS

FIRST MEETING WITH RAY

The year was 1976. Our fellowship at Wayside was rapidly growing in numbers from a small church of less than 100 in 1972, to a church which, by 1976, numbered 600 or so in attendance. The foundation was one of biblical exposition, teaching, and preaching through both the Old and the New Testaments. We had been strongly influenced through many individuals who were a part of the Bible Study Fellowship (BSF) movement with ministry headquarters here in San Antonio, Texas. Ray Stedman was on the board of BSF for many years.

We were a church body that, out of necessity, was moving more toward an elder rule form of government, with the congregation still having final authority. Most of us at the leadership level felt comfortable moving in that direction because the church was too big for congregational involvement in all issues to be practical. I remember a congregational meeting where we were to decide on a sign for in front of the church. After two hours of frustrating debate, while most members there expressed their individual opinions, the only option left was to hand it over to a committee. We knew that changes were necessary.

I had heard about Peninsula Bible Church (PBC), in Palo Alto, California, and its well-known teaching pastor, Ray Stedman. Who hadn't? The book Body Life was written by Ray and was one of the most popular books in the evangelical culture of the day. It was based on the body life of PBC. They hosted pastors' conferences for two weeks each year, and pastors came from all over the country. I was fortunate to be one of those pastors in 1976. It was the first time that I had ever been away from home, without my family, for such an extended period of time. But the time went quickly and was jam-packed with practical information on how to lead a church and how to preach and teach. Best of all was the quality time that was spent with the pastoral team, including Ray. They were completely available to each one of us. As I remember, there were fewer than two dozen of us in attendance. We were even allowed to sit in on the elders' meetings, just to see the inner workings of the leadership.

HIS MODEL FOR CHURCH LEADERSHIP

I came home with a number of convictions. First of all, it is the Lord's church and He will build it. There was a real trust in the Holy Spirit to bring unity and direction and to make things happen. I received the feeling that if the Spirit wasn't in it, it wasn't going to happen. Even the elders had to be unanimous in agreement if they were to move forward in any area of decision making. I was impressed with how the Spirit had led them.

Quoting from the biography on Ray, titled Portrait of Integrity, written by Mark S. Mitchell,

> He [Ray] believed the work of the ministry should be done by people in the pews rather than by the professionals and that the role of pastors is to equip the saints to use their spiritual gifts. In keeping with this conviction, Ray deplored all things ecclesiastical, even refusing to be called the senior pastor of PBC. He avoided anything that promoted hierarchical separation in the church, and he insisted that the church be led by servant-leaders (called elders) who were responsible to Christ, the Living Head of the body.[13]

Ray modeled servant-leadership.

In a message entitled A Pastor's Authority, he cites passages from the book of Acts dealing with a plurality of elders in each church. Then he makes this statement: "The point is no one man is the sole expression of the mind of the Spirit; no individual has authority from God to direct the affairs of the church. A plurality of elders is necessary as a safeguard to the all-too-human tendency to play God over people."[14]

This kind of thinking greatly influenced the direction that we took in leadership at Wayside.

Second, they were not into the numbers game. In fact, their desire was to start many other church plants throughout the Bay area. This they accomplished, in that many churches were planted and have flourished in that area. This became a model for us in the San Antonio area. Wayside has now planted eight churches in the greater San Antonio region. Each church was birthed in a different way. All had the blessing of the mother church. After all, it is His church and He can do as He pleases with it.

HIS MODEL OF BIBLICAL EXPOSITION

Third, the area where Ray might have had the most profound impact upon me was in the area of biblical exposition. He was a highly-respected Bible expositor. He was able to cast a spotlight on Scripture and make it shine. I loved to hear him open the Word. I loved to read his written messages. They influenced me more than I will ever know.

I had always been committed to preaching the Word. I knew that I wasn't smart enough to come up with good stuff week after week on my own. Whenever

I get compliments on a message preached, I will sometimes respond, "I have great material (all of Scripture) to work with." As pastors, we do have great material to work with. Shepherds are to be feeding their sheep.

Stedman was good at feeding the sheep. My dad had large dairy farms in north central Ohio. Prior to that, he had sheep. I remember going out to the barn and feeding and bedding down 600 sheep. I was only five or six at the time and probably more of a hindrance then a help. Years later with several hundred dairy cows, we had plenty of hired help. But my dad, a strong believer who was pleased that I became a pastor, reminded me over and over again to feed the sheep. In fact, some of his last words to me were, "Son, feed the sheep." He would say, "If there is feed in the barn, the cattle will come." Ray's ministry proved that axiom to be true. He modeled for us young shepherds (I was only thirty-three at the time) a good shepherd feeding his sheep. You feed them, they will come.

My time there became a benchmark for me. It was a recommitment to preach the whole counsel of God.

In the latter years of his life, Ray became concerned about the departure from strong, solid Bible exposition that he was seeing all over the country. So he became the catalyst for the formation of a new ministry called the Committee on Biblical Exposition (COBE). Many well-known Bible expositors from both America and England were part of this short-lived movement. We attended the COBE conference in Houston, Texas, held in 1987. It was one of the most encouraging conferences that I ever attended during all of my years in ministry.

> As the chairman for COBE, the last thing Ray wanted was just another conference on how to grow a church. He deplored church growth tactics. The whole purpose of COBE was to call churches back to what he believed was fundamental to their calling: the preaching of the Word of God, without which numerical growth was nothing but a fleeting and fleshly human endeavor.[15]

Up until the year in which he died, Ray continued to leave his marks on my life. When in the area, he would call me for lunch. I had the joy of playing golf with him. His golf game never measured up to his teaching. As a side note, when I first picked up golf here in San Antonio (through the help and encouragement of a professional golfer named Rick Massengale), I was very excited about this new sport. Then one day one of the Southern matriarchs in our church, who was very well cultured, said to me, "You cannot be a great preacher and a great golfer both." Well, Ray's golf game might have proved her right. But he played it with passion.

On his last visit with us, he shared with a mutual friend, Larry Heppes, and me that some physical tests which the doctors had taken concerned them. He was to have follow-up tests when he returned to his home. God took him home less than a year later. At his memorial service, many paid tribute to his life, including Chuck Swindol, Luis Palau, and other notable evangelical leaders who were personally discipled and influenced by Ray.

HIS MODEL IN DEATH

Mark Mitchell reveals in his book some wonderful and intimate and touching moments at the very end of his life. "Ray had a love for his Savior. More than anything, he wanted to see Jesus. When his daughter Linda, at his bedside, reminded him that he would soon get to talk with Moses and Paul, Ray responded, 'I just want to see my Jesus.'"

His home-going was quite remarkable, but just what you might expect from this stalwart of a man.

On October 7, Linda and Laurie (two of his four daughters) were at his bedside and Linda was reading from I Corinthians 15:50–55 (NASB). As she read those triumphant words, "Death is swallowed up in victory. O death, where is your victory? O death, where is your sting?" she and Laurie felt a holy presence in the room. And at that moment, Ray Stedman took his last deep breath and slipped away to glory. It was a fitting home-going for one who for so long had anticipated this day.[16]

Ray, you helped me in my marathon. You were there to offer me the Living Word and the Living Water along the way and to encourage me to keep on preaching the Word. I haven't finished yet, but with the encouragement of men like you, I have every chance of finishing well.

When Ray was asked how we, as pastors, can make a difference in the midst of a culture of decadence, he had a two-fold answer: first, we must give others "a model to follow, and second, we must give them a message to preach."[17]

Ray gave me, as well as others like me, a model to follow and a message to preach. That is what I desire to leave to others. I'm going to keep running. Thanks, Ray.

Defeat! He lay there silently, a
tear dropped from his eye.
"There's no sense running anymore—
three strikes, I'm out—why try?"
The will to rise had disappeared, all

hope had fled away; So far behind, so
error prone, closer all the way.
"I've lost, so what's the use," he thought.
"I'll live with my disgrace."
But then he thought about his dad,
who soon he'd have to face.
"Get up," an echo sounded low,
"Get up and take your place.
You were not meant for failure here,
so get up and win the race."

With borrowed will, "Get up," it
said, "You haven't lost at all,
For winning is not more than this—
to rise each time you fall."
So he rose to win once more,
and with a new commit,
He resolved that win or lose, at
least he wouldn't quit.
So far behind the others now,
the most he'd ever been,
Still he gave it all he had and ran as though to win.
Three times he'd fallen stum-
bling, three times he rose again,
Too far behind to hope to win,
he still ran to the end.
They cheered the winning runner as he crossed, first place,
Head high and proud and happy;
no falling, no disgrace.

But when the fallen young-
ster crossed the line, last place,
The crowd gave him the greater
cheer for finishing the race.
Even though he came in last, with
head bowed low, unproud;
You would have thought he won the
race, to listen to the crowd.
And to his dad he sadly said, "I didn't do so well."
"To me, you won," his father said.
"You rose each time you fell."

And now when things seem dark
and hard and difficult to face,
The memory of that little boy helps me in my race.
For all of life is like that race, with
ups and downs and all,
And all you have to do to win—is
rise each time you fall.
"Quit! Give up, you're beaten,"
they still shout in my face.
But another voice within me says,
"Get up and win that race."

Author Unknown[18]

CHAPTER SIX
THE WAY UP IS DOWN...
PHILIPPIANS 2:4–11

There is a consistent principle found throughout Scripture, and it is this: God humbles the proud, but gives grace to the humble. He knows how to bring down the proud and how to exalt those of a lowly heart. Proverbs 16:18 states it succinctly: "Pride goes before destruction, and a haughty spirit before a fall" (NKJV). Proverbs 29:23 reads, "A man's pride will bring him low, but the humble in spirit will retain honor" (NKJV).

Pride sets us up for failure. If we run our races well and finish successfully, we will do so out of a humble spirit. Pride keeps us from listening to God and from listening to others who can keep us running in the right direction.

HUMBLING MOMENTS

One of my most humbling moments happened just a couple of years ago. It seems that the older I get, the more those moments come my way. Connie has suffered from back discomfort due to curvature in her spine. I had seen the inversion tables advertised in infomercials on TV. It seemed to me to be just what she needed.

I was on a mission to have her try out an inversion table that suspends you upside down and takes the pressure off of your back. We have a sporting goods store a couple of miles away. So, it was near Christmas time, still quite warm here in San Antonio, and we went very casually dressed. I had on loose-fitting cargo shorts. The reason for this is that I love to fill my pockets with everything that I think I will need wherever I go. It is a sickness, according to Connie.

We arrived at the store and as we entered, there was positioned an inversion table no more than twenty feet from the main entrance. I took her over there and began to show her the features of the table and how it worked, as though I knew it all. I asked her to get on and see how it fit her. She assured me that she was not about to climb into it. I must go first and demonstrate to her how it is done.

So acting as though I knew what I was doing, I climbed up into the table, not realizing that the foot holders needed to be adjusted upward or downward according to one's height. Evidently, a little person had been in it before me. When I leaned back, it flipped me over in a fraction of a second and I was hanging upside down, suspended in the air, totally helpless. Worse yet, everything I had in my pockets began to empty out on the floor: keys, change, a knife, and whatever else

I had in them at the moment. There was no way that I could get upright. Furthermore, Connie was of no help. Remember, her back is the reason that we were there to begin with. In that brief moment, I was totally at the mercy of anybody that might help. My mind was racing with the question, "Who knows me that might be witnessing this humiliating moment in my life?"

Finally a couple of young men came over and helped me in my helpless plight. We have all had those moments of foolishness. Needless to say, it is a very humbling experience.

I have discovered that pride has been the underlying reason for nearly every problem I have encountered. Over the years I have tried to maintain a humble appearance. For many years I drove old pickup trucks. I was known and recognized for driving such unassuming machines. I loved to hear people talk about how humble I was. Here I was, the pastor of a growing, thriving church and yet driving old trucks. It just sounded so good to me to hear my name associated with humility in conversation. To put it more clearly, I was proud of my humility. So back in 2002, I decided to buy a new pickup, a 2002 Ford Explorer Sportrac. I soon discovered that I still had not extinguished my pride.

Max Lucado, pastor and best-selling author, known for his humility, tells of a similar moment of humbling in his own life. No one can say it quite like Max. Here is his story in his own words:

Deflating inflated egos is so important to God that he offers to help us. He helped me. I recently spent an autumn week on a book tour. We saw long lines and crowded stores. One person after another complimented me. For three days I bathed in the river of praise. I began to believe the accolades. All these people can't be wrong. I must be God's gift to readers. My chest puffed so much I could hardly see where to autograph the books. Why, had I been born two thousand years earlier, we might read the gospels of Matthew, Max, Luke, and John. About the time I wondered if God needed another epistle, God shot an arrow of humility in my direction.

We were running late for an evening book signing, late because the afternoon signing had seen such long lines. We expected the same at the next store. Concerned, we phoned ahead. "We are running behind. Tell all the people we'll arrive soon."

"No need to hurry," the store manager assured.

"What about the people?"

"Neither one seems to be in a hurry."

Neither one?

By the time we reached the store, thankfully, the crowd of two people had tripled to six. We had scheduled two hours for the signing; I needed ten minutes.

Self-conscious about sitting alone at the table, I

peppered the last person with questions. We talked about her parents, school, Social Security number, favorite birthday party. Against my pleadings, she had to go. So I sat alone at the table. Big stack of Lucado books, no one in line.

I asked the store manager, "Did you advertise?"

"We did. More than usual." She walked off.

The next time she passed I asked, "Had any other signings?"

"Yes, usually we have a great response," and kept walking.

I signed all the books at my table. I signed all the Lucado books on the shelves. I signed Tom Clancy and John Grisham books. Finally a customer came to the table. "You write the books?" he asked, picking up the new one.

"I do. Want me to sign it?"

"No thanks," he answered and left. God hit his target.[19]

He always does. It is not a matter of if, but when. It is a matter of time before the bottom falls out on us.

If humility is to be defined as not thinking less of ourselves, but rather thinking of ourselves less, then we can see that we all struggle with putting self before others. Pride is reflected in the words, "I will, not your will."

THE HUMILITY OF CHRIST

The reason that I love the Philippians 2:4–11 passage so much is that there is no finer statement made in all of Scripture to summarize the earthly attitude and ministry of Christ than what we have in these verses. There are even those who believe that the literary style of this beautiful passage might have been an early Christian hymn that Paul incorporated into his letter.

Here we have a stark contrast between the attitude of Christ and that of Satan, or Lucifer, given back in Isaiah 14:13–14. In that passage we see Lucifer just before his fall. His attitude is reflected in the words, "I will also sit upon the mount of the congregation, on the farthest sides of the North; I will ascend above the heights of the clouds, I will be like the Most High" (NKJV). Satan boasted about what he would do in ascending upward to be like the Most High. At the peak of his pride, God said to him, "You are going down. Instead of coming up, you are going down. You shall be brought down to sheol, to the sides of the pit."

Satan's attitude was, "I am going up. I will be like God."

The attitude of Christ was, "I am going down. I will empty myself of the glory which I had with Him."

Stuart Briscoe once heard Dr. Donald Grey Barnhouse speak at the Keswick convention in England. He surveyed the audience and then he said, "The way to up is down."

He waited for the crowd to settle and then he said, "The way to down is up." Briscoe looked at him and thought to himself, *That American preacher is a nut.* He switched him off that night and said that he was later sorry. He wrote, "Because if, as a kid, I could have learned that, I might have saved myself and others a lot of trouble."[20]

If we each had this attitude, how much better would our lives work? If we exalt ourselves and prefer ourselves in marriage, then our marriages will not work. Relationships cannot survive that way. Why is it that most Hollywood marriages do not work? It is for this very reason. Pride, demanding one's own way, destroys those relationships. Pride cuts us off from God and it cuts us off from intimacy in all other relationships. Pride is what motivates us to step out on our own and act independently. In our pride, we abandon God and step into sinning. This in turn brings failure and keeps us from finishing well.

I often reflect on the young pastor who was fresh out of seminary. He was serving his first church. Each Sunday he became more and more enamored with his own preaching. He listened too much to the accolades given to him. One particular Sunday he waxed quite eloquent, and then he heard the usual words of approval from his congregation. As he climbed in to his car, his head would hardly fit in the car door.

He was reflecting on how adept he had become at preaching when he said to his young wife, "Honey, how many great preachers do you think there are in the world today?"

Her response was classic: "I don't know, but one less than you think."

Let me say it again. The Scripture clearly teaches throughout this one great principle: "God resists the proud but gives grace to the humble."

"God sets himself against the proud, but he shows favor to the humble" (James 4:6, NLT). That same wording occurs in I Peter 5:5.

PRIDE PITS US AGAINST GOD

This means that we cannot win by ourselves. Life will not work. We are naturally in opposition to God. We experience His stiff arming. Sooner or later we will go through some serious humbling. King Nebuchadnezzar comes to mind in Daniel 4. This was probably the greatest example of God's humbling the proud, next to the passage on Satan. Nebuchadnezzar was the successful king in this vast empire of Babylon. His achievements had been unsurpassed in all of history. He was singing, "I've got the world by a string, sitting on the rainbow, got the little string around my finger, what a world, what a life." And then one day it all came crashing down on him.

It all came about through a dream. In the dream he saw himself as a great tree.

> The tree you saw was growing very tall and strong, reaching high into the heavens for all the world to see. It had fresh green leaves, and it was loaded with fruit for all to eat. Wild animals lived in its shade, and birds nested in its branches. That tree, Your Majesty, is you. For you have grown strong and great; your greatness reaches up to heaven, and your rule to the ends of the earth. Then you saw a messenger, a holy one coming down from heaven and saying, 'Cut down the tree and destroy it. But leave the stump and the roots in the ground, bound with a band of iron and bronze and surrounded by tender grass. Let him be drenched with the dew of heaven. Let him eat grass with the animals of the field for seven periods of time.
>
> Daniel 4:20–23 (NLT)

The terrible interpretation followed, which summarized, is this: Nebuchadnezzar would be humbled in his pride. He would live in the fields with the wild animals. He would be drenched with the dew of heaven. He would live like an animal for seven years.

Talk about humiliation, yet a year later he hadn't changed his ways.

> Twelve months later he was taking a walk on the flat roof of the royal palace in Babylon. As he looked out across the city, he said, "Look at this great city of Babylon! By my own mighty power, I have built this beautiful city as my royal residence and as an expression of my royal splendor."
>
> Daniel 4:28–30 (NLT)

That very same hour it happened. Just that quickly he was humbled. He lived this way until his hair was as long as eagles' feathers and his nails were like birds' claws. This great king was reduced to the appearance of a vulture for seven whole years.

Seven years later, his sanity returned to him. He praised the King of the heavens. Then he made this final observation: "All his acts are just and true, and he is able to humble those who are proud."

As pastors, pride can become our greatest downfall. If we begin to experience success and the ministry is growing in numbers and people's lives appear to be changing, we can, in subtle ways, begin to take the credit for it. We assume that there is something special about us. And like Nebuchadnezzar, many pastors have experienced this loss of sanity and humbling. It happens to all of us sooner or later. Like Nebuchadnezzar, we need to learn humility well. Don't miss this: the king says at the end, "My advisers and officers sought me out, and I was reestablished as head of my kingdom, with even greater honor than before" (Daniel 4:36, NLT).

God humbles the proud, but the reverse is also true: "He gives grace to the humble." Grace can be defined as undeserved favor or undeserved power and enablement. If we want His grace and power and favor, then we must humble ourselves.

Back in our text, we see the greatest example of self humbling.

HIS HUMILIATION AND HIS EXALTATION

We see His humiliation in Philippians 2:5–8. Think of this! Jesus was and is and always will be God. He was in the form of God. The Greek word for form is "morphe." This word means "the outward expression of the inward nature."

You have heard the saying "what you see is what you get." This is what we saw in Jesus. He was true to his nature. He was the real deal, the very God manifest in the flesh. As a pastor, I have always desired to reflect on the outside who I am on the inside. One of the greatest compliments that a wife can give regarding her husband is that what you see in the pulpit is what he is in private.

There was no doubt about Jesus' eternality and oneness with the Father: "In the beginning the Word already existed. He was with God, and he was God" (John 1:1, NLT).

And we cannot miss what John meant by the expression "the Word," for in John 1:14 we read, "So the Word became human and lived here on earth among us. He was full of unfailing love and faithfulness. And we have seen his glory, the glory of the only Son of the Father" (NLT).

In John 10:30, "The Father and I are one" (NLT).

The great "I AM" statements in John's Gospel are the claims of Jesus to His deity.

Paul gives a beautiful summary statement in 1 Timothy 3:16 of what is being taught here in Philippians 2: "And great and important and weighty, we confess, is the hidden truth—the mystic secret—of godliness. He (God) was made visible in human flesh, justified and vindicated in the Holy Spirit, was seen by angels, preached among the nations, believed on in the world and taken up in glory" (AMP).

We know that He had a glory with the Father before his incarnation. In John 17:5, He prayed, "And now, O

Father, glorify Me together with Yourself, with the glory which I had with You before the word was" (NKJV).

He gave up that glory temporarily as He came down in human flesh to this planet. He never stopped being God, but He did stop exercising some of His privileges of being God. It was a huge step downward. When man set foot on the moon, we heard astronaut Neil Armstrong proclaim, "One small step for man, one giant leap for mankind." That might be a bit of an exaggeration as we look back over the past four decades. But we do know that when Christ set foot on this planet it was one great step downward for One, in order that we might take one huge leap upward.

During His sojourn here, He did not hold on to who He was or cling to it. As the New Living Translation renders the phrase in verse 7, "He made himself nothing." The Greek word "kenoo" appears only four times in the Greek New Testament and it refers to nullifying something or making it of no account.

HIS OWN DID NOT RECOGNIZE HIM

He disguised Himself of His true identity. A recent book by Mike Yankoski, entitled Under the Overpass,[21] gives the account of two young men who gave up their belongings, status, pride, relationships, influence, affluence, sense of well-being. and even risked their health in order to live among the street people in cities such as Denver, Washington D.C., Portland, San Francisco, Phoenix, and San Diego. That gives us some feel for the idea that is expressed here in Philippians 2:5–8.

When we were ministering at a missions conference in Japan in 2006, I took on another identity one night. Missionaries love to have fun and they know how to do it. I had spoken to the group for several days. The last night was fun night. Now it was my turn to have some fun. That night I got up from the front and went back into the men's room and put on my Scottish hat, which had long, red hair hanging from the rim, my black-rimmed glasses with a long fake nose, and my Billy Bob teeth which needed some major dental repair. I came back in and sat down toward the back. First the children were turning around looking at me and not knowing what to say. They got the attention of their parents who, in turn (casually), looked back and weren't quite sure what they were seeing. They all concluded that it was one ugly man in their midst. I had been their speaker, but they did not recognize me at first. Jesus came as their Messiah and yet Israel did not recognize Him.

When you disguise yourself, you cannot change your real identity. I was still the same person. Jesus was the same. He was God. Yet He became the servant of humanity. The Sovereign One became the servant of all.

If we catch the full impact of this passage, it will translate into our daily conduct in the home, the church and the marketplace. We have all encountered people at times who have been given a bit of authority and they flaunt it. They use it at every opportunity. They can make life miserable for the rest of us. It might be a supervisor who loves to lord it over those under him or her, or a policeman who goes too far with his authority, or even a pastor who uses his exalted position as a weapon over his home and over his congregation. He fails to live down to being a servant-leader.

I was preaching at a pastors' wives conference in the Ukraine several years ago. I made the statement that if we offend our wives or treat them wrongfully, we must ask their forgiveness. After the session, one of the pastors wanted to see me privately. He argued that if he asked forgiveness of his wife, it would diminish his authority. I said, "To the contrary: it will elevate your stature in her eyes."

When we humble ourselves, God exalts us. Jesus reminded the disciples that they were not to be like the Gentiles, "lording it over others" (Matthew 20:25–28).

I often think that if I had the kind of power available to me that resided in Him, I would have used it thousands of times over the years to get even when others have wronged me. You know, when someone cuts you off in traffic, have you ever had the urge to blow out all four of their tires to slow them down a little? That is our sin nature. Jesus could have abused His power, but He did not do so.

One of the great problems in churches today is the attitude of senior pastors lording it over their staff and congregation. This lack of humility poisons the entire church and community. I often wonder what our homes, neighborhoods, cities, states, and countries would be like if we all had the attitude reflected in these verses.

Peter reminds his readers in I Peter 5:5–6,

> Likewise you younger people, submit yourselves to your elders. Yes, all of you be submissive to one another, and be clothed with humility for God resists the proud, but gives grace to the humble. Therefore humble yourselves under the mighty hand of God, that He may exalt you in due time. (NKJV)

Clothing is one of the first things that we notice about one another, especially when it comes to ladies. Peter is reminding us that our humility needs to have that kind of visibility. In that atmosphere, God can work and great things can happen in relationships and ministries.

—

His exaltation in verses 9–11 follows His humiliation. This is always the way it goes. First the humbling, and then comes the exalting. The "therefore" reminds us that because Jesus humbled Himself, God exalted Him.

His name is above every name. One day, every person will bow before Him and (verbally) acknowledge with their tongues that Jesus Christ is Lord. That moment of inevitability is coming.

The very fact that men curse in the name of Jesus today bears witness to His name being the highest name. Can you imagine hearing someone curse in the name of Buddha or Mohammed or some other familiar religious figure? Why Jesus? Because whether men who use His name in vain understand why they do it or not, they are affirming His name to be above every other name.

His greatness is reflected in His many names. One name cannot begin to define who He was and is. Throughout history there have been many religious figures who gained a following. They had one or two names at the most. But Jesus had many names. Furthermore, the whole theological discipline known as the doctrine of Christology has resulted in hundreds and thousands of books that have been written trying to understand this Unique One who was both fully God and fully man. There is no study of Buddha such as Buddha-ology. And the followers of Mohammed have no discipline known as Mohammed-ology. They were common ordinary men like each one of us. But Jesus, the God-Man, is unique.

Why is there such an all-out effort today to discredit Scripture and undermine the deity of Christ? It is because His name is above every name. He represents absolute truth. He is absolute truth (John 14:6). No matter how hard men may try, they will not be able to change the truth. Truth always wins out.

Why is His name above every other name? The text makes it clear that He humbled Himself, even to the point of death. And for this cause, God highly exalted Him and gave Him a name above every other name.

We often use the name "Christian" to describe who we are. But that designation has fallen on hard times in some parts of our world. One of the missionaries (whose identity needs to remain anonymous) that Wayside Chapel supports in the Arab world made the comment about how the name "Christian" has such a negative connotation in many parts of the Arab world. It is because of all of the evil misdeeds often affixed to the Christian faith. The Middle Age Crusades are usually cited as the prime example. But even today, the smut and filth produced in Hollywood, the break-up of American families and the drug culture that seems to be winning the battle for the minds of some of our choicest youth, all is packaged from this allegedly "Christian" nation. He said that Arabs don't want that. Too much baggage is associated with the name "Christian." But he said, "If you ask them if they would like to become a follower of Jesus, then the response is often quite different." Jesus is incredibly attractive, but far too often His followers are not. And one of the great traits that makes Jesus so attractive is His humility.

It is interesting that the word "disciple" occurs over 260 times in the New Testament. The word "Christian" only occurs three times.

Of course, to humble ourselves and bow before Him voluntarily now means salvation. To be forced to bow before Him at the Great White Throne Judgment in Revelation 20:11–15 means condemnation.

Years ago I memorized a poem which, to my knowledge, is anonymous. I wish I could give the person credit for it. It is a good one. It has been a motivator in keeping me in the race, running for the goal. It is entitled "The Judgment Seat of Christ":

When I stand at the Judgment Seat of
Christ and he shows me his plan for me,

The plan of my life as it might have
been, had he had his way and I see,
How I blocked him here and I checked him
there and I would not yield my will,
Will there be grief in my Savior's eyes,
grief though he loves me still.

He would have me rich, but I stand here
poor, stripped of all but his grace,
While memory runs like a haunted thing
down pathways I cannot retrace.
Then my desolate heart will well nigh
break with tears that I cannot shed,
I will cover my face with empty hands, I
will there bow my uncrowned head.

Lord, of the years that are left to
me, I give them to thy hand,
O take me and break me and mold me
to, the pattern thou has planned.

Author Unknown[22]

There is something special, both terrifying and comforting, about the name of Jesus. Are you allowing His mind of humility to be in you?

CHAPTER SEVEN

MEET RUSSELL KELFER—"NOT I, BUT CHRIST"

It was two years after arriving at Wayside Chapel that God brought Russell and Martha Kelfer into our lives. I had heard much about them and the ministry they had to single students and young adults. In fact, they had weekly meetings in their home where Russell and Martha hosted around 150 the last year or so. The group was drawn together by Russell's teaching and the warm atmosphere of Martha's hospitality.

THE BEGINNING OF OUR MINISTRY TOGETHER

The Kelfers visited and started attending Wayside in 1974. We had added on to our original sanctuary space in 1974, doubling the seating capacity to nearly 300. We averaged 100 or so in attendance at the time before its completion. That Easter Sunday of 1974 we had 250 in attendance. I had resigned myself to believe that we would never see that many again. Our EFCA denomination consisted primarily of small churches, of 100 or less. By 1976, we were averaging 600 in attendance. Russell began teaching in 1977 and, before long, had several hundred in his Koinonia class.

As a pastor, when you have someone like Russell

coming to your church, you need to put him to work in the ministry. He was a unique writer and story-teller. He had some training in journalism from the University of Texas (UT), but was uniquely gifted in a way that few of us will ever be. He was able to bring the principles of Scripture to light through practical application. He had a way of putting words together and structuring his thoughts that kept your attention focused, even though he was reading his lessons from manuscript. In later years, the transcripts were passed out to each member in his class for each person to follow along while he was reading it. Russell also had a gift for poetry. You will notice a number of his poems have been included at the end of quite a few chapters in this book.

I recognized that giftedness and what Russell could bring to the ministry that I never could. I was not threatened by him, but I understood that teaming up with him and allowing him the freedom to exercise his gifts would only bless our ministry and make us look better. So for twenty-three years, from 1977 until 2000, we worked side by side, never getting in each other's way, never crossing each other's paths, but rather embracing and enhancing one another. It was amazing how many times, without consulting one another, our messages blended and complimented each other. Both his ministry, Discipleship Tape Ministries (DTM), and my ministry at Wayside were blessed through this long-term relationship.

Russell not only had his own taped messages going out around the world, but his ministry was also sending out my taped messages and those of others who occasionally preached from our pulpit.

HUMOR ALWAYS HELPS

One of the greatest practical jokes ever pulled on me was done by Russell Kelfer. One day Russell sent me a tape with the title "A Collection of Steve Troxel's Greatest Jokes." I have been known for my good and bad jokes. People at Wayside were very tolerant and understanding. I was complimented later in my ministry that as I got older my jokes were getting better. It's great that something improves with age.

I thought to myself, This is so nice of my good friend to go back over the years and glean all of my best jokes and put them on a single tape for me and for my posterity. I could hardly wait to get out in my old pickup truck and slip that tape into my tape deck (the good old days of tapes) and be amused by my best jokes. I remember slipping it in and turning it on and increasing the volume. I was driving down the freeway by the front of our church. But there was no sound. I fast-forwarded it a little further, and still no sound.

I finally had it fast-forwarded to the end of the tape and still there was nothing. I thought to myself, It must be on the other side. I turned it over and started listening. Still, there was only silence. Then I realized that he had pulled a really good joke on me. That is one that our people will never forget. He loved to have fun. He could give it out and take it just as well.

MAKING THE MOST WITH WHAT HE HAD

Russell had some physical limitations. He only had one eye. His other eye and one ear were damaged at birth. And then that same damaged eye was totally destroyed in a compulsory PE class in which he was assigned to handball. He was hit in that eye. Great pain ensued and never lessened. Doctors eventually removed the blind eye. But for some unknown reason, for the rest of his life he continued to have pain in his good eye. I remember the night when I was rooming with him at the UCLA campus, where three of us had attended a seminar. He took his glass eye out and sat it on the table between our beds as we retired. I felt like the eye of Texas was upon me all night long. He was a loyal UT fan as well. He had only one eye and only one good ear, but he made the most of what he had and he persevered in ministry through a lifetime of pain.

Every pastor should be so fortunate to have a Russell Kelfer ministering side by side with him for many years.

In recent years here in San Antonio, we have had two notable basketball players who are numbered among the top fifty all-time greatest players in the NBA. You may recognize their names: David Robinson (now retired), and Tim Duncan, in the midst of a very successful career. As good of an athlete as David Robinson was, he was never able to be successful in bringing home an NBA crown without the help of Tim Duncan. When the opportunity came along to have Tim as their number one draft pick in 1997, David welcomed the opportunity to play alongside Tim. He even allowed Tim to overshadow him in many areas. What David had not been able to do on his own in all the previous years, he was now able to do in 1999 and 2003. Now Tim Duncan is having equal success, but he is quick to compliment his teammates, without whom he could not win the NBA's most prized trophy.

There is a great leadership lesson here: there is no limit to what we can accomplish if we surround ourselves with good people and work as a team. In business, all successful CEO's understand that their success is largely determined by the staff that serves with them. Together they can reach the top. It is true in all areas of life and ministry. At the leadership level, we looked for the three C's, not original with us by any means. I am not even sure where I first heard it. It may well have come from Bill Hybels. The three C's are character, competency, and chemistry. For teams to get along together they need to have all three. Russell was that kind of a man and teacher. He had character. He was competent in so many ways, but like the Apostle Paul, he was quick to acknowledge his inadequacy and that his sufficiency was of God (II Corinthians 3:5). And he also enjoyed good chemistry with the rest of the team.

HIS VALUE AS A TEAM PLAYER

Here are some reasons I valued Russell as a team player:

1. When we were facing tough decisions, he was one to whom I would go for counsel. I can remember two occasions, separated by years, when larger, more prestigious churches in other parts of the country approached Connie and me about considering their senior pastorates. Most offers that came our way were easy to decline. But two intrigued me. Maybe it was the timing, the issues that we were dealing with, or the temptation to move on to something bigger and grander. I made my way to Russell. He would pray and then each time returned with the

counsel, "Not now: your ministry is not finished at Wayside." So I stayed the course. We each need someone like that who will give us some honest perspective and help us keep our feet on the ground and our necks in the yoke.

2. Russell understood the exchanged life, where it is "not I, but Christ," (Galatians 2:20) living and working through me. It is not what we can do for God, but rather what He wants to do through us. I cannot say that I learned the concept through Russell, but it was certainly reinforced in his teaching. This emphasis permeated our church and every decision that we made, including operating with a "no debt" policy. We wanted it to be so big and impossible that only God could accomplish it. Russell strongly challenged us in that vein.

Russell's life was eternally-focused. He led by example. He "waited for that city which has foundations whose builder and maker is God" (Hebrews 11:10, NKJV). Russell challenged all of us to live for the eternal.

HIS IMPACT IN DEATH

God took Russell home quite suddenly in early 2000. He was hospitalized for what most of us thought would be a routine medical procedure on his heart. But God had other plans for Russell while he was on the operating table.

On the night of his memorial, the church was filled with people coming from all over the country to pay tribute to this unassuming and unpretentious man who allowed Christ to live His life through him and give Him the glory.

The following Sunday, I put aside what I was planning to preach and gave a message on the impact of Russell's life. It is not often that a pastor feels led to do this. This was the first and only time in forty-two years of ministry that I did this for one of our own. His impact was great indeed.

I spoke on a text from II Timothy 4:

> For I am already being poured out as a drink offering, and the time of my departure is at hand. I have fought the good fight, I have finished the race, I have kept the faith. Finally, there is laid up for me the crown of righteousness, which the Lord, the righteous Judge, will give to me on that Day, and not to me only but also to all who have loved His appearing.
>
> II Timothy 4:6–8 (NKJV)

That was a fitting tribute to this humble servant. He was ready. He had fought. He had kept the faith. And he had finished his race.

And while he was fighting and running, he kept me in the fight and in the race as well. Thanks, Russell! Your life made a wonderful difference in my life and in the lives of many around the world.

The legend is told that many years ago, during the fighting of a battle, a certain captain did great things with his sword; he accounted for scores of the enemy's deaths and his deeds became known throughout the army and were reported to the king. At the end of the engagement, the king sent for that sword. "Let me see this sword that has done so much. Bring it to me," he said. They brought it to his majesty, and he gave it back with an air of disappointment. "It is an ordinary sword: I see nothing special in it." He returned it to the captain. They told the captain what the king had said, and he ventured to send back this message: "You should have sent for the arm that wielded it."[23]

It's not the sword: it is the arm that wields it. Russell could not have agreed more. Russell was simply the sword. All glory goes to the one who wielded him.

"Why God Chose Me..."
by Russell Kelfer

My talents? Is that what he saw long ago?
My talents? I see that the answer is "No."
My looks? Just a mirror dispels that thought.
If that's why he called me, he called me for naught.

My wisdom? Not even a trace do I see.
Then why? Tell me why did my Saviour call me?
And just like the wind as it glides through the sky.
A voice softly answers, "Yes, I'll tell you why.

"Because, when I looked, you were nothing to see,
And when I shine through noth-
ing, then men will see me.
I call men of weakness, so I can be strong;
I call even the downcast and give them a song.

"I call out of nothing; so when something appears,
Men give ME the glory, and
down through the years,
It has been so, though the world is appalled:
Not many noble nor wise have been called."

The poor man, the weak man,
though often despised,
Come alive at God's touch, and
the world is surprised.
The fruitless, the failures, the dregs of the earth,

Become princes and kings when
God's Son gives them birth.

And in spite of their past, or how they were raised,
God gives them life, and the world is amazed.
Your credentials for heaven? I'll give you a clue:
They're only that God has found Jesus in you.
In spite of your weakness, your failures, your health;
In spite of your lack of applause, praise or wealth;
He called, he equipped, he sent from above,
And made you his chosen, and bathed you in love.

Twas only that God, in his infinite power,
Gave us himself in that marvelous hour,
When we said, "Yes," to his gift of grace,
And Jesus said, "Yes," as he took our place.

What a trophy we are; what a victory indeed!
(But not for our value, but rather our need.)
Then let's yield all we are, all we have, all we own;
Relinquish our pride, and come
down from our throne,

And turning to Jesus, let's worship and praise
That he will be Lord all the rest of our days.
My talents? My wisdom? No, dear God, now I see,
It was grace, and grace only that
you should choose me![24]

CHAPTER EIGHT
IT'S ALL ABOUT HIM
ISAIAH 6:1–8

Isaiah 6 has made its mark in my life and has kept me running throughout my life, especially over the past several years. I have gradually come to the realization that life is not about me. I am not a quick study on some of these things.

This chapter places us in the year when Isaiah saw the Lord. Brennan Manning is the author of a book called Ruthless Trust. In it, he shares from the movie Waking Ned Devine. A ten-year-old boy asks the interim pastor of his church, "Do you ever see God?"

"Not directly," says the young pastor, "though I get revelations."

"Does your job pay well?" inquires the boy.

"No. The rewards of my work are mostly spiritual."

Then the pastor asks the boy, "Have you ever thought about a life of service to the church?"

"Not really," he says. "I don't want to work for someone I never see and who doesn't even pay minimum wage."[25]

How about you? Isn't that something that we all struggle with? Life would be so much different if we could just see Him and hear from Him directly. His written Word is great, but we would love to hear His voice.

This is what the prophet Isaiah experienced. It came at the most difficult time in his life. For it was "in the year that King Uzziah died that I saw the Lord sitting on a throne" (Isaiah 6:1–3). What Isaiah was about to see and hear touched him so deeply that he was never the same after that encounter. He was already a believer. He was a prophet. He knew God.

ISAIAH MADE READY FOR A DIVINE ENCOUNTER

Some background on Isaiah is helpful here. He was born of nobility, born Isaiah Ben Amoz. He was a recognized statesman, having access to the royal court of his day. He counseled and rubbed shoulders with princes and kings. He was well-educated. He was not some kind of a looney belonging on a funny farm, speaking about some hallucination that he had. We hear people today talking about revival, barking like dogs, hopping like frogs, laughing like hyenas, roaring like lions, and hooting like owls. But there was none of this with Isaiah. This was the real thing: a genuine revival through a close encounter with the God of the universe.

I contend that all genuine revival follows this pattern, we see the Lord in His holiness, and then we see ourselves in our sinfulness, and finally we see others in their neediness.

King Uzziah was one of the better kings who ruled over Judah. He became king when he was only sixteen years of age and reigned for the next fifty-two years. He brought great stability to the land of Judah. Contrast this with our own country. In the past fifty-two years, we have had ten presidents, from General Eisenhower to President George Walker Bush. A good number of the people of Judah were born and died under the reign of King Uzziah. He was all they knew.

Unfortunately, he did not finish well. In the eyes of the people, he had done no wrong. But in God's eyes, he had committed a grievous sin involving his pride. After he acquired great wealth and power, like many in places of power, he began to think that he was above the law. But in his case, he violated the laws of God. He boldly entered the temple and arrogantly assumed priestly powers. When the priests tried to stop him, he became enraged. In the midst of his rage, leprosy broke out on his forehead. He ended his days living in a separate house, being a leper, cut off from the house of the Lord (II Chronicles 26:21).

In spite of this, when he died, it was a time of deep mourning. It was a time of great national uncertainly. It was the end of an era. What did the future hold? Isaiah probably went to the temple to get some answers. He wanted to hear something from God about the future. He received much more than he had hoped for.

Have you noticed how it is often in times of sorrow and tragedy that God meets with us in fresh, new, and revitalizing ways? The year 1963 was a memorable one for me. God had called me into the ministry in 1957. But I must admit that I had thoughts about rejoining my dad and two brothers back on the farm. Connie and I had attended a Bible college in the South for the first year and a half after high school. When we returned home for the holidays at the end of 1962, we discovered that my mom had an advanced case of breast cancer. She had kept the information from us during the fall semester, but could not keep it hidden any longer. So we decided to go back to college and finish the semester in early January, and then come back home to care for my mom and my younger brother and sister and to try to help my dad where we could. Mom died on April 7, 1963, and it shook my world. I guess, even at that point in my life, I had never looked at the mortality of my own parents, let alone my own life. I was living in a state of illusion. Others were dying, but I never thought much about the death of those close to me. This forced me to think deeply about death and life after death. On top of that, a close friend of my parents, who did some carpentry work for my father, stopped in almost daily to check with my dad, but also to share the latest radio message from some of the Bible teachers on radio at the time. Suddenly, our friend died of a heart attack. That too was another reminder to me of the brevity of this life.

Then the really big one came on November 22nd of that year, when news spread quickly around the nation concerning the great tragedy that took place in Dallas, Texas. Our youthful president had been assassinated in the prime of his life. Though I was not a great fan of the president at the time, I could not help but feel deep sorrow for the Kennedy family and for the rest of the nation. We watched the events in Dallas unfold, along with the swearing in of President Johnson aboard Air Force One as he returned to Washington. It was a time of great uncertainty. Was this a conspiracy? Was there more to come? I don't know about you, but for me it was one more reminder that year that life is very temporary, at best.

My parents had a framed poem hanging over the stove in the kitchen. It went like this: "Only one life, 'twill soon be past. Only what's done for Christ will last." This was a wake-up call, and for me, it was time to experience the Lord's presence and call all over again.

Later, another poem I heard stated the same truth:

"The clock of life is wound but once, and no man has the power, to say just when the clock will stop, at late or early hour. Now is the only time you own to do His precious will. Do not wait until tomorrow for the hands may then be still."

Yep, it was time for me to get back in the race. I transferred to Detroit Bible College, later becoming William Tyndale College, for the next semester beginning in January of 1964. And I have never looked back.

So I can similarly say, as Isaiah, that it was in the year that my mother died and the president was assassinated that I had my encounter with and a renewed call from God.

This long-time king Uzziah, the well-respected king of Judah was dead. But when Isaiah entered the temple, he encountered the real King. The real King was very much alive, and on His throne and about to make His presence real to Isaiah.

There are three things that Isaiah saw in that temple.

ISAIAH SAW THE LORD

First, he saw the Lord. The word for Lord is "Adonai." The word means "master" or "Sovereign One." This was a title that was reserved for God alone. It was also the title that was given to Jesus in the New Testament. We have titles and names today. Over the years, some would call me "Pastor" and others would call me "Steve." And some have even called me less flattering names. And when my wife gets irritated with me, she refuses to use the term of endearment that we have used with each other over the years, "dear." It becomes "Stephen," a very formal name. And on rare occasions, I have heard "Stephen Phillip," with my middle name. I played a practical joke on a friend, Larry Heppes, one day and he called me "maggot." That was the only time that I can recall where I was blessed with that designation. One of Job's counselors, Bildad, in Job 25:6, referred to man as a maggot and a worm. Steve is my name. Pastor is my title.

God has many different names. Jesus has many different names and titles. But "Lord" speaks of who He is in title. He is the Sovereign Lord of the universe. He is the one who is controlling all things. He is reigning. He is the real King. Kings and presidents and prime ministers and their administrations will come and go, but the real King lives forever and "of the increase of His government and peace there will be no end" (Isaiah 9:7, NKJV).

The interesting truth behind this passage that is often overlooked is that the One whom Isaiah saw in this passage was none other than a pre-incarnate appearance of the Lord Jesus Christ. In John 12:38–40, John is quoting from this sixth chapter of Isaiah. Then, in John 12:41, we read: "These things Isaiah said when he saw His glory and spoke of Him" (NKJV). There it is clear that he is speaking of Jesus.

The title "Lord" speaks more of His transcendence. The name "Yahweh," which meant the covenant-keeping God of Israel, speaks of His immanence. God is both transcendent and high and lifted up above us, and at the same time He is immanent, very much interested in what is going on in our personal lives.

Years ago, a popular song said it so well. The title of the song was "How Big Is God?" The words were, "How big is God, how big and wide his vast domain, to try to tell, these lips can only start. He's big enough to rule His mighty universe, yet small enough to live within the heart."[26]

Isaiah saw Him "high and lifted up, and the train of his robe filling the temple." All of this speaks of His awesome transcendent power, His majesty and royalty. King Uzziah, in his finest hour, could not hold a candle to the real King who is seated upon the throne.

Several years ago, we had a private tour of Air Force One, while Bill Clinton was president. One of the young men from our congregation, Everett DeWolfe III, son of the elder Everett and Ruth DeWolfe, served as the navigator on Air Force One for two presidents during his thirteen year tour of duty. I remember walking all through the plane and even sitting down behind the desk in the flying oval office where the phone, hanging next to the desk, gave the president immediate contact with many of the great world leaders. It was a brief, fleeting feeling of power. But nothing can compare with the kind of power that Isaiah felt, being in the presence of the All-Powerful One. This was the real control room in the universe.

Isaiah was used to being in the presence of kings and other dignitaries, but he had never seen anything like this. He was associated with princes and kings. He knew what it was to be surrounded by greatness and in the presence of greatness.

Back in 1994, we were invited to the inauguration of George W. Bush as governor of Texas. We attended a prayer breakfast where there were perhaps 250 to 300 invited guests, mainly pastors and spouses. Governor Bush stood to address those gathered and then said that there was somebody else that he wanted to introduce us to. Out from behind the curtain stepped his father. Needless to say, I was impressed with being in the presence of a governor and former president, along with elected senators from Texas, including other dignitaries. We were no more than fifty feet away from the platform. I would still be impressed today in the presence of such figures, but not nearly as much as in my younger days. Age does bring wisdom and puts things into much better perspective.

Isaiah saw the "seraphim" above the temple. The word "seraph" means "burning ones." The two wings covering their faces were probably doing so in order to protect them from being scorched by the blinding presence of God. The wings would act as a shield. Seeing the sun is a reminder of this Blazing One. The sun's temperature is reportedly 27 million degrees Fahrenheit at its core and 10,600 degrees Fahrenheit at its surface. To look directly into the sun with the naked eye would scorch the retina. This is part of the reason why God has said that no one can look at Him and live. We talk about a scorched earth policy. If He did not keep His distance from us, we would be disintegrated into ashes in a nanosecond.

Often when God appeared as recorded in the Old Testament, He did so in the form of fire. In Hebrews 12:28, we are to "serve God acceptably with reverence and godly fear. For our God is a consuming fire" (NKJV). Fire is one of the most destructive forces known to man. According to II Peter 3, God will destroy this present earth and heavens by fire. And He will create out of the ashes a new heavens and a new earth. New life will come from the old just as we have after a forest is burned. Time replenishes what was burned.

The fact that the seraph covered his feet probably speaks of self-humiliation. How else could lesser beings respond in the presence of the Great One?

With two wings, the seraph also flew. This speaks of the mobility of the angels to move quickly to carry out the will of the Great One on His throne.

"And one cried to another and said, 'Holy, holy, holy is the Lord of hosts; the whole earth is full of His glory!'" (Isaiah 6:3, NKJV).

The repetition of the word "holy" is for emphasis. The writer doesn't want it to be missed. Holiness is what God is by nature. He alone is holy. Holiness is what separates Him from His creation. Holiness is perfection in all of His attributes. In fact, the words "holiness" and "wholeness" come from the same root word. To become holy is to become whole. God is in the process of making us whole. I Peter 1:15–16 reminds us of this great truth: "But as He who called you is holy, you also be holy in all your conduct, because it is written, 'Be Holy, for I am holy'" (NKJV).

It is hard to define, but we know it when we see it, for we melt in its presence. The "whole earth is full of his glory." The Hebrew word for "glory" is "kabod," and is rich in various shades of meaning. It was used in reference to one's worth: his wealth, silver, and gold. It was also used of one's position: his eminence, power, and authority. A third meaning would be His divine and terrible radiance. In the words of an old Jewish epigram, "God is not a kindly old uncle, He is an earthquake."

That becomes clear in verse 4, where the posts of the door were shaken by the voice of him who cried out, and the house was filled with smoke. This ground was made holy by the presence of God.

This opened the eyes of Isaiah to something else.

ISAIAH SAW HIMSELF FOR WHAT HE WAS

Second, he saw himself. He became acutely aware of his own sinfulness and shortcomings (Isaiah 6:5–7). An encounter with the holiness of God brings us to the end of self- thinking and selfish praying. It is no longer about us. We discover that we are not the center of the universe. He is! Not only was the temple shaking, but Isaiah was shaken to the very core of his being. His personal universe disintegrated. His feelings are verbalized in verse 5: "Woe is me, for I am undone [destroyed, cut off]" (NKJV).

We don't use the word "woe" anymore in conversation. It was frequently used in Scripture. The Hebrew word is "Oi." It was a pronouncement of doom. Isaiah saw himself as doomed. Peterson's The Message translates it, "Doom! It's doomsday! I'm as good as dead."

The word "undone" means to be coming apart, breaking up. It is similar to having an emotional breakdown. Today we would want to medicate him, or maybe even put him in a straight jacket and haul him away. Here was a man who once had it all together, but now sees it all coming apart.

An evangelist friend, Sammy Tippit shared that revival is not the top blowing off, but rather the bottom dropping out.

For Isaiah, the bottom dropped out. He saw his own filthiness. He makes reference to his own unclean lips. He was broken up over his own uncleanness and the uncleanness of the people around him.

I remember as a child hearing about one of the great revivals that swept this country and produced this kind of response. One who longed for revival was heard leaning against a lamppost in New York City crying out, "O God, the sin of this city is breaking my heart."

This was a moment for the reorienting of Isaiah's moral compass. He was no longer comparing his own morality with the people around him.

Isaiah was all too familiar with the sin of Uzziah. Perhaps he was comparing himself with the great king and he came out looking pretty good. There may have been some self-righteousness that needed to be eradicated from his life. We evangelicals had a tendency to do that with President Clinton. We found the nature of his moral failures involving many women to be revolting and disgusting. In contrast, we looked pretty good next to him, in our own eyes.

But Isaiah now had the perfect standard of holiness before him and he became vividly aware of his own sinfulness. Until we encounter God, we will never weep over our own sins or the sins of society around us.

Why did Isaiah feel this way? He explains it in verse 5: "For my eyes have seen the King, the Lord of hosts" (NKJV).

Years ago, our church choir had a party at a local country club. It was advertised, at least to Connie and me, as a '50s party. So we did as we were told and dressed up like we did back in the '50s. But there was a problem. Once we arrived there, we discovered that we were the only ones told that it was a '50s party. All others wore black tuxes, ties, and evening gowns. It was a great practical joke on us. How did we feel? We felt very out of place. We were very self-conscious. We felt that those who were not part of our group but just coming and going from the club must have been looking at us and thinking to themselves, Why would those people ever come to a black tie function dressed like that?

This is how we feel when we are confronted by His awesome holiness. We are overwhelmed by our own sinfulness. We feel terribly out of place. Isaiah did not feel fit to be in His presence.

But one of the seraphim took care of the problem as stated in verse 6. He flew over to Isaiah and touched his mouth with a live coal, which he had taken with the tongs from the altar.

God burned his uncleanness away, like using a gamma knife pointed toward the cancer within. We hear it expressed so many different ways, but the bottom line is that God must first work in us before He can work through us.

ISAIAH SAW OTHERS

Third, Isaiah saw others (Isaiah 6:8). You cannot see God in that way and see yourself in this way without seeing others in a whole new way. This is why genuine revival among believers always results in a great tide of evangelism, bringing countless multitudes to Christ.

A new burden for others brings with it a new boldness. If we could visualize the future nightmare of the countless numbers of people in eternal punishment, separated forever from the Great Giver of life, many of them our friends and next-door-neighbors, we would have a whole new burden and boldness.

God then speaks, saying, "Whom shall I send, and who will go for Us?" (NKJV). Isaiah has a whole new sensitivity to the call of God.

Isaiah was quick to respond, "Here am I! Send me." The New Living Translation renders it, "Lord, I'll go! Send me."

God cannot use us until we come clean and are broken before Him. In the movie The Horse Whisperer, I recall the scene where the trainer, played by Robert Redford, breaks the horse down to its knees, in order that it might learn submission. I had a local rancher once tell me that if the horse is too difficult to break they will sometimes tie the legs of the horse together and take it down on the ground. Then they will throw a blanket over the head of the horse and leave it alone for a time. The horse must feel abandoned. But it is all for the purpose of breaking it in order that it might be made useful. Sometimes the procedure has to be repeated several times before the animal is broken.

God must do the same with us. Are there times when you feel as though God has tied your arms and legs, allowed you to go down, and has just thrown a blanket over you and walked away from you? You might feel as though He has abandoned you and forgotten about you. But He could never turn His back on His own. It all has a divine purpose.

Supposedly A. W. Tozer has written that "it is doubtful whether God can use a man greatly until He has hurt him deeply."

In Isaiah 57:15, we read: "For thus says the High and Lofty One who inhabits eternity, whose name is Holy: I dwell in the high and holy place with him who has a contrite and humble spirit, to revive the spirit of the humble to revive the heart of the contrite ones." The New Living Translation reads: "I refresh the humble and give new courage to those with repentant hearts."

I have come back to this passage many times over. It has kept me in the race. I realize that there must be the constant renewing through confession. When that happens I begin to more clearly see the needs of others around me.

How about you? Where are you in the race? If you have a broken heart, you are in a good place. God is preparing you for something great.

I thought I understood how holy God can be.
The very thought of holiness, I
thought would set me free.

I thought by seeing God as holier than I,
My bleak horizons, somehow,
would broaden like the sky.

Until Isaiah six, one day, began to sink within,

And I began to see my God in light of all my sin.

The angels gathered round his
throne of holiness did sing;
Louder, louder, "Holy, Holy" did their chorus ring.
And as their music touched my
heart, no matter how I tried,
I could barely say the words: "I am unclean!" I cried.

Deeper, no, the Spirit went, until with heated coal,
He burned the concept "holiness" into my very soul.
"Now you see yourself, my child,"
my Jesus said to me,
"You are a filthy sinner; now you can be free."

With that, he placed upon my lips
that burning, fiery coal,
And said, "Now go in peace, my
grace has made thee whole.

Now I can send you, child of
mine, into the battle's din,
For you have seen a Holy God, and
you have seen… your sin."4

CHAPTER NINE

MEET BILL COSE—A MAN OF FAITH AND ENCOURAGEMENT

Every man needs another man to run with him when it comes to long distances. When I first started running back in January of 1975, I needed a running buddy to motivate me. I had been to my doctor, who told me that I needed to do something aerobically to keep myself in good health and to help control my weight. I read one of Dr. Ken Cooper's books on aerobics. The motivation was there. But I needed someone to run with to keep me accountable. I tried running with others for the first few years, but schedules often kept that from happening. Then running became a necessity for me. Today I still run, but alone.

Whom do you have running alongside of you? Bill Cose was that kind of a man with me. When I think of Bill, two words come to mind: encouragement and faith. I first met Bill back in the summer of 1973 at our Evangelical Free Church conference in Green Lake, Wisconsin. I remember the warm reception he gave me into the Free Church. He and his wife, Mildred, had been serving pastorates in the Free Church in the Western U.S.

THE BEGINNING OF OUR MINISTRY TOGETHER

A few years later, Bill and Mildred moved to San Antonio after hitting a bump in the road in a church in California. They had a couple of daughters and their families living here. It was to be a time of healing for them. What was California's loss was our gain in Texas.

Our church warmly received them and it was only a matter of time before Bill was selected to become one of our elders. Since he was a pastor, twenty-one years my senior, and more seasoned then me, I was naturally drawn to Bill. Bill was honest with me and, at the same time, always encouraged me. Each one of us needs that kind of a father figure in our lives. More than once I referred to Bill and Mildred as a mom and dad to me. I really did feel that way about them.

Recently, at the beginning of 2007, God took Bill home after a long and fruitful life and ministry. He went home rather suddenly while still serving as a pastor on staff at Wayside Chapel.

Let me fill in some blanks for you. Bill began teaching in the public school system here in San Antonio, but he also had a great ministry at Wayside. As an elder, he often would give needed insight as a man of faith, at just the precise time needed.

AN EXAMPLE OF FAITH

For example, back in 1985 we were bursting at the seams, having three services on Sunday morning and in need of a larger facility. At the same time, well-known pastor John Hagee, of Cornerstone Church, was building a new facility north of San Antonio, along Highway 1604, known as the outer loop. They had outgrown their old facility, located along Highway 410, the inner loop. They were offering it to us at a cost of $2,400,000. It had an auditorium that would seat somewhere between 1,200 to 1,400 people. It was just what we needed for a congregation that numbered around 800–1,000 at the time. But the cost of the facility seemed prohibitive at that time for a congregation our size. There was another small problem. Our congregation had a "no debt" policy that was traced back to a couple of years after Connie and I arrived at the church. A number of us at the leadership level came to that conviction. We agreed that it was not unbiblical to borrow money, but at the same time we were going to trust God to provide our needs beforehand rather than afterwards.

Cornerstone needed a buyer and we needed a larger facility. It seemed like a win-win situation for both of us. It was a huge step of faith for us. Here was the plan. We would put $100,000 in escrow. Cornerstone would give us two years, until October of 1987, which was about the time that their new facility would be completed. If we did not have all of the money in hand by October of 1987, then the deal was off and Cornerstone would walk away with the $100,000. But, for fiscal reasons, this was not what they wanted. They wanted to see us succeed. It was an exciting time for both churches. Both congregations were praying that God would provide.

Here is how God provided for us and where Bill Cose comes into the picture: we encouraged our people to make a faith pledge. We asked them to pray and consider what God would have each family unit give, over and above their normal giving. We asked them to write the amount on a slip of paper, without the name, and put it in a little wooden box that would be kept locked until the day of reckoning. We did not want to jeopardize our giving to missions, both local and overseas. A large percentage, even up to 60 percent of our general fund, was going to missions at one point. We had to adjust that downward to pay our bills at home. We now had a sizable full-time staff, which required a larger portion of each year's budget. God was going to have to pull this off. Dwain Rogers, a corporate executive in our congregation, said to me at the time something like this, "I have put a pencil to this and there is no way that we can come up with the money."

During one of our elders' meetings, one of the newer elders, Ted Skeans, much younger in the faith, asked the question, "What is our contingency plan if the money isn't there on the date of closing?"

Bill Cose whirled around, looked at him, and said, "Brother, we don't have a contingency plan. God will provide."

And provide He did. Cornerstone took our old property on Vance Jackson Road off our hands, so the amount of money to be raised was now closer to $2,000,000. It was still a huge mountain to climb. The first year, the giving was slow. During the second year, the momentum began to build. Our people were giving checks large and small. During the Christmas Eve service of 1986, a man stuck an envelope in my pocket that contained a check for $50,000.

Just a word of encouragement for pastors here: I tried to stay as far away from the finances as I could. But at times like this, I found that it was extremely difficult because the givers of large sums of money wanted to make sure that I knew, for encouragement or to see that the check was properly handled, or whatever their motives may have been. One Sunday morning an older couple in the church placed a $100,000 check in the offering and our ushers nearly had a heart attack.

On another day, a rancher, who had made significant amounts of money in the oil business, called and wanted to be sure that I was in the office. He wanted to stop by and give a donation to the relocation fund. It was another check for $100,000.

One day, a man who had been blessed in the real estate business called and told me how God had led him and his wife to the figure of $100,000. They didn't know how God was going to provide it, but they believed that He would. He was really excited when he discovered that a property that he had planned to sell was now closing on the same day that we were to close on the church property. He wanted us to send him a deposit slip to the bank account of the church and he would make the deposit on that same day. We had an elders meeting and I notified them that the money was now in. But they insisted that it is not in until it is in. That was wise counsel.

On the day of closing, I had a phone call from another couple in the church. The wife asked me how much money we still needed. I said $14,000. She said that her husband's secretary was on the way over with a check that would more than cover the shortfall. It was a check for $26,000. There was great rejoicing over God's provision. And I want to add that it took everyone's giving, both large and small gifts, to get us there.

When the faith pledge box was opened, we discovered that the total amount pledged was way short of what was needed, only $1,400,000. Of that amount, one family had pledged $400,000. In the final analysis, by 1987 they were in chapter 11 and were able to help very little.

Now, remember the real estate couple? We still had not heard from them. A week went by and he called and quite apologetically said that he was sorry about the delay. An easement issue had hung it up on closing day, but the issue was now settled and closing was now finished. He was depositing the money promised in the church account that same day. On top of that, another $50,000 plus came in. What was the reason for the delay? God knew that we would need $150,000 more to refurbish the facility. There was a need for renovation, including new carpet and paint in this well-used facility.

And then you might remember that later that same month the stock market plummeted. As one man who made significant gifts toward the project said to me, "If closing had been a month later I would probably not have had the money to give." God's timing is perfect, always.

THE GREAT ENCOURAGER

Now, back to Bill Cose. He was so instrumental in

keeping us on track, walking by faith and not by sight. A couple of years later, Bill retired from the public school system and moved back to California. We had a need for a pastor who would visit the hospitals and lead the seniors. We called the seniors the OWLS (Older, Wiser, Loving Saints). Bill responded to the call, and for the next sixteen years, we ministered side by side again. My office was only twenty feet from his office. During the darkest moments of my life, Bill was there. When we went through a couple of moral failures at the leadership level, Bill was there for me to help bear the burden. When the church finances were down and I was a bit discouraged, Bill would step into my office and say, "Look at the track record, brother. God always provides." And he was right, as usual.

While others might complain about the insufficiency of pay in ministry and opt out for more lucrative careers, Bill would say, "Isn't this great, brother? I love what I am doing and even get a paycheck for it. It doesn't get any better than this."

I was rooming with Bill at the Promise Keepers Pastors' Conference in Atlanta in 1996 when the phone call came that their precious daughter Vickie had cancer. We knelt together and prayed at our beds. His faith was unwavering.

We had many funny moments together as we ministered at dozens of funerals over the years. We saw just about everything go wrong that can go wrong at a funeral. In one particular funeral, I was to simply speak. I had no part in the planning for the service leading up to my sermon, which always makes me nervous. It was a tragic accident involving a young executive in a Middle-Eastern country. The funeral home was packed. It was a totally secular funeral, so bizarre that I will not try to describe it to you. Words were spoken that should have never been spoken in a mixed audience, especially while trying to eulogize the dead. I had to speak following all of the frivolity. There was a spiritual wall that was there that day. It was very difficult to get up and bring some semblance of sanity back into the room. I began by pointing to the corpse in the open casket and said, "This is reality. We are all going to die. This is not the end of life. We are all going to be somewhere after we die. The question each one of us must answer for ourselves is this: 'Where will I be one moment after I die?'"

Bill was in attendance, but not part of the service. After the service he met me out in the parking lot to encourage me. He put his hands on my shoulders and looked intently into my eyes and said, "Brother," as he shook his head, fishing for encouraging words. Words didn't come, but plenty of laughter did. We both started laughing so hard that we nearly collapsed on the pavement in front of the funeral home, hopefully oblivious to the mourners who were filing out to their cars to proceed to the cemetery.

There were plenty of moments like that with Bill. Every pastor needs an older, seasoned pastor to encourage him along the way. Bill kept me running. He kept me laughing. He finished his race of eighty-five years. Well done, Bill! He went home with his boots on. He passed on to better things with his faith firmly rooted in Christ.

Bill understood that God was doing his fighting for him.

"The Battle Is Not Yours"

Thousands and thousands of years ago,
God's people prepared for a test,
As the Ammonites and the Moabites
descended, destruction their quest.

But Jehoshaphat saw the problem, and
we read from God's precious Word,
That "Jehoshaphat prepared a fast
and prepared to see the Lord."

And all the people, young and old,
gathered together that day,

And humbled themselves before the
Lord as Jehoshaphat started to pray.

He lifted his voice in remembrance,
recalling the days of yore,
And promised that God would keep his
word as always he'd done before.

And finally, in utter abandonment,
he spoke these words so true:
"We have no might against them,
Lord, nor know we what to do!"

Then, from the very lips of God, there
came these words sublime:
"Fear not, my precious children; the
battle's not yours. It's mine.

"No need to fight, beloved, here's all you need to do:
Just take your place, stand still and see,
your God will fight for you."

So they bowed their heads and wor-
shipped, and appointed men to sing;
Not to fight God's battles, but to let his praises ring.

Here comes the enemy, now sing!
Let every voice be raised.
God's people start to shout and sing,
and lift their hearts in praise,

And when their lips in praises sang,
lo, then, the job was done.
God, at the sound of their voices, fought,
and at once, the battle was won.
Now what about you, dear Christian; in
your heart, have you seen the light?
Have yet you come to understand
the battle's not yours to fight?

That all your precious Jesus is longing for you to do
Is to set yourself stand still, and see
that he can live through you.

The battle's not ours, oh, shout it!
The battle's not ours to win.
The battle belongs to Jesus, and
Jesus will reign from within.

Acknowledge you cannot do it, and
begin to sing and praise,
And God will begin to fight for you as
you humbly acknowledge his ways.

No, the battle's not ours, beloved.
The battle belongs to the Son.
The battle's not ours, but the victory's
ours, and the victory's already won![27]

CHAPTER TEN
WE ARE AT WAR
EPHESIANS 6:10–20

We have used the metaphors of racing and running to describe the Christian life. But there is another metaphor that is also used quite frequently in the New Testament. It is warfare. We don't run very long until we discover that we have an enemy. I believe that millions of times a day in millions of believers around the world, Satan wins a victory and the Christian suffers a disastrous defeat, simply because of not being prepared for warfare.

Recently Connie and I were privileged to participate in the annual gathering and celebration of the Dolittle Tokyo Raiders, which was held here in San Antonio. Connie was asked to sing the National Anthem, and I was asked to do the invocation. Many are unfamiliar with that part of history. Five B25's took off from the SS Hornet aircraft carrier out in the Pacific on April 18, 1942, and headed toward Tokyo loaded with bombs. It was a one-way mission. Each plane had sixteen men aboard for a total of eighty. Of the original eighty, only fourteen survived, and of the fourteen, only seven were able to attend the convention here in San Antonio this year. The fate these men suffered is the subject of many books. Dolittle did little to determine the outcome of the war. But the Japanese military was caught by surprise. They did not think that they were vulnerable to our attacks. It was somewhat demoralizing to their national pride and psyche.

Of course, in our own country, we remember our own day of infamy, December 7, 1941, when the Japanese surprised us at Pearl Harbor, and a more recent attack September 11, 2001, when terrorists caught us off-guard as they struck the Twin Towers in New York City.

Enemies in times of warfare always want to use the element of surprise on their opposition forces. It is extremely critical that we know the power available to us and the power of the enemy. Some of us are so beaten up while we are reading these words that we hardly know what happened and who is to be held responsible.

Lt. Gen. Romeo Dallaire, Force Commander of the UN Assistance Mission to Rwanda during the horrific genocide in Rwanda during 1994, was an eye-witness to the horrendous massacre. He writes, "In just one hundred days over 800,000 innocent Rwandan men, women and children were brutally murdered while the developed world, impassive and apparently unperturbed, sat back and watched the unfolding apocalypse or simply changed channels." He continues, "After one of my many presentations following my return from Rwanda, a Canadian Forces padre asked me how, after all I had seen and experienced, I could still believe in God. I answered that I know there is a God because in Rwanda I shook hands with the devil. I have seen him, I have smelled him and I have touched him. I know the devil exists, and therefore I know there is a God."[28]

We just recently (2007) had a pastors' wives conference in Rwanda that brought together 400 senior pastors and wives from six different countries and eighteen different denominations. What Satan sought to destroy, God is restoring and renewing.

WE DO HAVE AN ENEMY

We may not be able to see him with our physical eyes, but we are able to see, smell, and touch him as we experience his evil all around us. Perhaps the unseen forces of terrorism, lurking around the world, or even pockets of terrorist cells right here in our own cities and neighborhoods are the best illustration of the unseen forces of evil that Paul mentions in verse 12 of this passage:

> For we are not wrestling with flesh and blood—contending only with physical opponents—but against the despotisms, against the powers, against the master spirits who are the world rulers of this

present darkness, against the spirit forces of wickedness in the heavenly (supernatural) sphere.

Ephesians 6:12 (AMP)

The enemy—the devil—and his unseen forces of evil are constantly stirring up conflict within us and among us. He shows up in the home, in your place of business, and in the church. And he strikes when we are least expecting it.

I think of the anecdote of the man at Halloween time who decided to masquerade as the devil and visit a local church during one of their services. As he entered the church people screamed and spread out trying to evacuate the auditorium as quickly as possible. They fanned out in various directions. But one little old lady down in the front never moved. He came and knelt down and blared out in front of her face, "Aren't you afraid of me?"

"No," she shot back.

"Why not?" he said. "I am the devil."

She responded: "I am not afraid of you because I know who you are. I have been married to your brother for the past fifty years."

We need not be scared of the devil if we understand who he is and his subtle ways and tactics of attacking us.

When we are experiencing many conflicts with others, we must understand that oftentimes the real enemy is not our wife, husband, child or parent, supervisor, employer, colleague, your pastor, your elders, your teacher, or anyone else in the body of Christ. It is with the enemy himself.

William Gurnall, the Puritan commentator, has a wise and insightful word on this:

> When reproached and persecuted by others, look beyond them. Send your wrath on Satan, who is your chief enemy. Men are only his puppets. They may be won to Christ's side and so become your friends at last. Anslem explains it in the following manner: "When the enemy comes riding up in battle, the valiant soldier is not to get angry with the horse, but with the horseman. He works to kill the rider so that he may possess the horse for his own use. We must not bend our wrath against the deceived, but against Satan who rides them and spurs them on. Let us pray fervently, as Christ did on the cross, that the devil will be dismounted and these miserable souls delivered from him."[29]

We know from Matthew 16:21–23 that Satan can appear through the closest of friends. Jesus had just told the disciples of His coming suffering, death, and resurrection.

Then Peter took Him aside and began to rebuke Him, saying, "Far be it from You, Lord; this shall not happen to You!" But He turned and said to Peter, "Get behind Me, Satan! You are an offense to Me, for you are not mindful of the things of God, but the things of men."

Matthew 16:21–23 (NKJV)

Jesus identified the real enemy. This attack was not coming from Peter. Peter had no awareness that Satan was speaking through him. Sometimes our closest friends can say the most hurtful and harmful things, without even being aware of it. The enemy uses the comments to discourage us and bring us down to defeat.

The devil always does his dirty work behind the scenes. He never shows up physically or visibly. He never announces his arrival on the scene. This is why his very existence is made light of and is fodder for jokes by standup comedians. But there is no other satisfactory way to account for all of the evil that is in the world and the evil that touches our lives apart from the presence of an evil one.

He is always there lurking in the shadows. He is as "a roaring lion, seeking whom he may devour" (I Peter 5:8, NKJV). Back in 1990, we visited a wild game park while we were ministering in South Africa. We went out on early morning and late evening safaris. We watched lions stalking their prey. They were very patient and looked for the weakest and most vulnerable animals to attack. Then, at the opportune moment, they would launch their full scale assault.

What must we do? How can we protect ourselves? Paul answers that question in Ephesians 6:10–20.

WE CAN DEFEAT OUR ENEMY

First, we must be strong in the Lord (Ephesians 6:10). This is the first command, a present, imperative verb. It is also a passive verb. It means to allow the Lord to strengthen you. Always be strong in the Lord and in the power of His might. The New Living Translation renders it, "A final word: be strong with the Lord's mighty power."

We must make sure that our relationship with Him is strong and intimate. Like sheep staying near the shepherd, the predatory animals will not attack. They are always safest nearest the shepherd. Up north in the wintertime, we had a game that we would play called "Fox and Geese." We would clear paths in the snow that would form a wheel with spokes going out from the hub in the center. There was one fox, but everyone else was a goose. The geese were safe as long as they remained in the hub or the center. When they wandered from the hub, they were fair game for the fox. The idea was for the fox to catch all of the geese outside of the hub. Of course, to make the game fair, none of the geese could remain in the hub indefinitely.

This also means that we must never trust our own strength. Remember the words of that great hymn, "A Mighty Fortress is our God," by Martin Luther? One verse goes like this, "should we in our own strength confide, our striving would be losing. Were not the right man on our side, the man of God's own choosing. Dost ask who that may be? Christ Jesus, it is He, Lord Sab-a-oth His name. From age to age the same, And He must win the battle."[30] We don't have enough strength to fight him. We all know the story of David and Goliath. David said to Goliath:

> You come to me with a sword, with a spear, and with a javelin. But I come to you in the name of the Lord of hosts, the God of the armies of Israel, whom you have defied… all of this assembly shall know that the Lord does not save with sword and spear; for the battle is the Lord's, and He will give you into our hands.
>
> I Samuel 17:45–47 (NKJV)

It is imperative that we operate in His strength and not rely on our own.

WE MUST PUT ON THE ARMOR THAT HE HAS PROVIDED FOR US

We must operate in his strength and we must take up the armor that he has provided for us. "Put on the whole armor of God that you may be able to stand against the wiles [schemes] of the devil" (Ephesians 6:11, NKJV).

We must delay no longer. We must do it with haste. Some of us have ignored the armor far too long. We cannot afford to wait any longer. The days are becoming increasingly evil.

Knowing what we must do is not the same as doing it. Remember the ridiculous story about a group of animals in the jungle who decided to have a football game? The problem was that no one could tackle the rhinoceros. Once he got up a head of steam, he was unstoppable. When he received the opening kick-off, he rambled for a touchdown. The score was seven to nothing almost immediately. Somehow, they managed to keep the ball away from him the remainder of the first quarter. At the beginning of the second quarter, the other team tied the score seven to seven. The lion tried to warn the zebra on the kickoff not to kick it to the rhino. But the zebra ignored the warning. The rhino caught the ball and he was going for a touchdown. Suddenly, from out of nowhere, he was brought down with a vicious tackle. When the animals un-piled, it was discovered that a centipede had made the tackle.

"That was fantastic," roared the lion. "But where were you on the opening kick-off?"

The centipede replied, "I was still putting on my shoes."

Many of us are like the centipede, only we are still trying to decide if we need to put the armor on. We are not sure that we really need the armor. We may arrogantly think that we can take on the enemy without it. We do not see the danger. In the meantime, we are losing the war against him.

The command here in verse 11 to "put on the whole armor of God" is in the aorist tense. It is a once and for all putting on of the armor. It is not something that we are to put on and then take off and put on and take off. Put it on and leave it on.

The same word occurs back in 4:20–24, where we are commanded to put off the old man, the former conduct, and "put on the new man which was created according to God, in righteousness and true holiness" (NKJV).

We have the same idea in Romans 13:14: "But put on the Lord Jesus Christ and make no provision for the flesh, to fulfill its lusts" (NKJV). The imagery is that of putting on clothes. One of my least favorite pastimes is purchasing clothes. It occurs only when I am in the mood, and that is seldom. I don't like the effort of going into the dressing room and taking off and putting on. It does require energy and effort. This is why so many of us have been slow to put on the armor. It requires effort and discipline.

To excel in the physical realm requires lots of discipline, effort, and staying power. The same can be said in the area of academics. Most students, in order to excel, must spend hours of disciplined study before taking the test. You cannot sit down at your desk and pray, "Please, Father, give me complete recall of all the things that I have never studied." We quickly discover that those prayers will not be answered in a positive way.

The same can be said for the military. Some never survive basic training. To be a good soldier requires great discipline and conditioning. Why is it that we expect things to just drop in our laps spiritually, and every day become more like Jesus, and experience greater victory over the enemy and yet we are not willing to discipline ourselves toward godliness?

WHY WE MUST PUT ON THE FULL ARMOR

The whole purpose of this equipping is that we "might be able to stand against the wiles of the devil." Standing is always a posture of victory. One of my favorite scenes in the book of Revelation is in chapter 5. There is One who is found worthy to claim the title deed to earth. He is the real possessor. John looks in verse 6 and, "behold, in the midst of the throne and of the four living creatures, and in the midst of the elders stood a lamb as though it had been slain" (NKJV). The Slain One is now standing, announcing His mighty victory over the evil one. When two boxers go at it, oftentimes there is only one that is left standing. He is proclaimed the victor. To hold our ground against our foe and still be standing, we must arm ourselves. I take great comfort in Paul's words in II Corinthians:

> But we have this treasure [the gospel] in earthen vessels [clay pots] that the excellence of the power may be of God and not of us. We are hard pressed on every side, yet not crushed; we are perplexed, but not in despair; persecuted, but not forsaken; struck down, but not destroyed [we get knocked down, but we get up again and keep going, NLT] always carrying about in the body the dying of the Lord Jesus, that the life of Jesus also may be manifested in our body.
>
> II Corinthians 4:7–10 (NKJV)

Verse 10 comes alive in The Message: "What they did to Jesus, they do to us—trial and torture, mockery and murder; what Jesus did among them, he does in us—he lives!"

The enemy wants to knock you down and keep you down. He will do everything in his power to keep you from standing. The "wiles of the devil" in Ephesians 6:11 refer to his scheming craftiness. The Greek word is "methodia." We get the word "method" from this word. He has many different methods.

First, he will do everything in his power to keep you from trusting Christ for salvation. "But if our gospel is hidden or veiled, it is veiled to those who are perishing, whose minds the god of this age has blinded who do not believe, lest the light of the glorious gospel of Christ, who is the image of God, should shine on them" (II Corinthians 4:3–4, NKJV). You might be reading this book and it occurs to you that you have never trusted Christ for salvation or you have doubts about your relationship with Him and where you are going to spend eternity. The desire of the enemy is that you will continue to be blinded to the gloriousness of the gospel message. C.S. Lewis reminds us that Satan doesn't say there is no hell. He just states that there is no hurry.

Second, once we have trusted Christ for salvation, the enemy will try to keep us from trusting Christ for daily living. He would have us striving in our own strength. He knows that we are no match for him.

When we are trusting in ourselves to get it done, we end up tripped up in sin, and perhaps our testimony is rendered ineffective.

HOW THE ENEMY ATTACKS US

Ephesians 6:16 speaks of the flaming missiles that he is always sending in our direction. The purpose of a missile is to hit and destroy its target.

I Timothy 3:7 and II Timothy 2:26 both refer to "the snare of the devil" (NKJV). A snare was something that a trapper would use to catch a wild animal. Satan sets his traps, just like the coyote with the roadrunner, but unfortunately, is far more successful. It might be an enticing business deal, too good to be true, or a beautiful woman who makes it clear that she is interested in you, or a handsome man who is understanding and attentive, or a drug that is promised to put you on a high and make you feel better. It might be the temptation to strike back and get even, to destroy another person's reputation. It can be sinful thoughts and actions from the past for which Christ has already forgiven you. But the enemy brings them to the surface again.

Good hunters always keep themselves hidden. It is amazing to me to see the way we outfit ourselves for hunting here in Texas. I have been on hunting trips where hunters equip themselves with all kinds of arsenal, weapons, dogs, vehicles, and the latest gadgets in helping them find and shoot their game animals. A friend who once went with us quipped that we are as well equipped as some third world armies. But the number one issue in hunting is to keep yourself hidden. Camouflage clothes are designed for both hunters and the military. Satan does a masterful job in keeping himself hidden.

Fisherman, likewise, keep themselves from being seen. I have been down fishing at the Gulf of Mexico with friends. Chartered boats and professional fisherman will never drive over the top of a school of fish. No, the professional fisherman will skirt around them. He stays a distance away, out of sight, and casts the line out to where they are.

Hunting, fishing, and fighting in time of war all have the same urgency: to remain hidden. A hunter uses feed or will imitate the sound of his prey to bring them in. A fisherman will use a hook (covered, of course) with a juicy-looking worm on it. The purpose is to deceive and catch what he is after.

Satan is the master deceiver in our lives. Jesus referred to him as the ultimate and consummate liar, "the father of lies" (John 8:44, NLT).

He will come to us in our moment of greatest weakness. In the case of Jesus, Satan waited until after he had fasted for forty days and was hungry. His first temptation concerned food. He said to him, "If you are the Son of God, command that these stones become bread" (Matthew 4:3, NKJV). Jesus knew what to do and say to remain standing. "It is written, man shall not live by bread alone, but by every word that proceeds from the mouth of God" (verse 4). He relied upon the Word of God. So must we.

Satan and his cohorts in evil study our weakness just like hunters and fishermen scrutinize what will appeal to their prey. He will make appeals to us based upon what he finds. One of my weak tendencies has been to become discouraged. Sometimes when I have been in that condition over the years, I would get a critical letter or comment made that would pretty much flatten me. He knows that I am most vulnerable to criticism when I am discouraged and tired.

He will even get us to question the Word of God about what it has to say about the consequences of the sinful actions that we are about to engage in. Eve was fully aware that God said to her that she was not to eat of the tree from in the midst of the garden or she would die. Satan responded, "You will not surely die.... your eyes will be open and you will be like God, knowing good and evil" (Genesis 3:4–5, NKJV).

Satan desires that we step out of our dependency

upon God, so he appeals to our pride. And our pride sets us up for failure.

There is an old Native American Indian legend where each young brave, when coming of age, would have to do something that no other brave had ever done. This particular brave stepped out of his teepee one morning and looked around, scoping the landscape, contemplating what he might do to prove that he was a man. As he looked toward the tallest range of mountains, he realized that none of the other braves had ever climbed to the top. So he decided this was his moment. He took his warm buffalo hide and Indian blanket and began his way toward the mountains. It took him days to reach the top, and when he finally scaled the last peak, he was swelling with pride. He was thinking to himself, I am finally a man. I have done what no other brave has ever done. All of a sudden, he heard some rustling at his feet. He looked down and before he could react he heard a voice saying, "Young man, would you please pick me up and take me back down to the bottom of the mountain? It is cold up here. This is no place for a snake."

The young man looked at the beautiful creature and realized what he was dealing with. He responded, "Oh, no, you are a poisonous snake. You will bite me and your venom will kill me."

The snake quickly responded, "Oh, no, young man, with you it will be different. We will have a special relationship. I will not hurt you."

The more the young man listened and looked, the more he was persuaded. He picked up the creature, put it under his warm hide under his arm and proceeded to take it down the mountain to the green meadow below. When he arrived at the bottom, he gently lifted the snake down to the ground. At that moment, the snake coiled and flew into action, striking the young brave in the calf of his leg. The young brave cried out, "But you promised me!"

The snake responded, "But you knew what I was when you picked me up," as it slithered off into the grass.[31]

Might I ask you the question: What are the snakes in your life that are potentially lethal and deadly?

Are you listening to the voice of the enemy without regard to the consequences of your own sin at the other end? James reminds us that lust leads to sin, and sin, when it is finished, brings death (James 1:13–15).

"Hath God Said?"

"Hath God said?" the serpent chirped,
"Did he say... 'Don't touch'?
Or did he simply mean, 'Now Eve,
please, don't eat too much'?"

"Hath God said?" the devil cried,
"What right hath God to tell
Any man or woman that they'll be doomed to hell?"

"God hath not said," said Satan
(a lie man soon believed).
And when he did (and when we do)
we've simply been... Deceived![32]

CHAPTER ELEVEN

MEET AN UNKNOWN PREACHER IN NORTHERN BURMA

This chapter is written to pay tribute to an unknown pastor in Northern Burma, now Myanmar, who in one brief contact and in one sentence gave me a new perspective on the final leg of my marathon. But before speaking about him, allow me to share with you what took me to northern Burma in January of 2004.

OUR TRAVEL TO BURMA

In the mid-1990s, our church began to focus on missions in that area, concentrating in Thailand, which is the next-door-neighbor of Burma. We have had teams of doctors and dentists who have regularly gone to that area to train a group of men and women, called the Barefoot Doctors, to go from village to village dispensing medicine, pulling teeth, and doing whatever else may be needed.

We also helped fund a medical clinic in the remote village of Patau in the north, including some expensive equipment needed for good medical procedures. And in the process, a couple of sawmills were built and many in our church, including the children, helped raise the money to purchase an elephant. You say, "Why an elephant?" Logs were cut from the jungle and floated down the river to the location of the sawmills. The elephant was then needed to pull the logs from the river and drag them up the hill to the sawmills for the final leg of their journey.

Over a period of time, many houses were built, along with church buildings, a Bible college, and other buildings. The government wanted their percentage of time from the sawmills so they could build housing for their military and build bridges making these remote places more accessible. Because Wayside had contributed so much in these various endeavors, the government of Myanmar, through its top general who was then leading the country (but has since been overthrown), invited us to come and celebrate the twenty-fifth anniversary of the Barefoot Doctors ministry. Thirteen of us left the states and met up in Rangoon. It was once we arrived there that I was informed that I was the first preacher from the West to be invited and allowed to preach in North Burma in forty-two years. We were escorted quickly through customs and put on a military transport to Patau, with two other stops along the way. We saw God answer prayer as it related to the weather clearing and the sun coming out again, just long enough for us to make the last leg to our final destination. The Christians in Patau were praying that the rain would stop and the weather would clear. At the very time they were praying, we were able to take off in the plane, make the final flight, and land safely. When we arrived safely, the rains resumed. Their faith so greatly encouraged us.

We stayed in a military compound and were under the watchful eye of the military wherever we went. They were there for our protection, but also to observe. Persecution of Christians is commonplace in the northern part of this country. We had a couple of young ladies from the government who served as government monitors, regularly sending updates on our activities back to the central government.

The celebration was to take place in a remote spot, across a fairly wide river, about one hour each way from where we were sleeping. It was a very rough ride in the back of trucks that were used to transport soldiers. This had all been arranged by the Christians with the government before our arrival. Some of the road was so muddy and rutty that tractors had to be used to pull the trucks through these places.

An unforgettable moment occurred as we crested the hill and saw the river. On the other side, we could see crowds of the native peoples, both of the Rawang and Lisu tribes. Many had on their tribal dress and headgear. They had various instruments that they were playing. The only thing that separated us was a temporary (and fragile-looking) bridge made with lumber from the sawmills. The bridge spanned a swollen river that was probably 100 yards across. When the rainy season would come, the river would swell even more and sweep the bridge away. But for now it was ours to use.

We continued our way across the bridge and were treated like dignitaries by the large crowds. We made our way to a spacious field the size of several football fields in the village where a bamboo structure, containing a thatch roof, but open on all sides, had been built. It was large enough to have around 3,000 people seated on the floor inside with lots of standing room on the outside for another couple of thousand people, or more. The crowd was estimated to be about 5,000 in attendance for the two days of meetings. The meetings started at 10:00 a.m. and lasted until 4:00 p.m. or so. Since the emphasis of the conference was on reaching out, I preached a couple of messages on our motivations for missions. I challenged them by explaining to them that now that they had heard the Gospel, they were charged and responsible to work together in evangelizing the rest of the villages in their areas.

During those six hours of meetings each day, of which I only preached for an hour or so, I was amazed at the perseverance of the people. Very few moved or had to get up and use the outdoor facilities. They sat transfixed on what was being seen and heard from the front platform. They were hungry for the Word, to say the least.

When the two days of conferences were concluded, two moments stuck out in my memory. The first one occurred when we were walking back to the house where our final meal at the conference was being prepared and served. A number of the pastors followed us. It was now dark. They had a fire burning in a courtyard outside. We sat around the fire. There were a dozen or so pastors sitting around the fire just looking at me like I was from another planet. There was no translator through which we could communicate, so we sort of smiled and nodded at one another. Then I asked someone to find a translator. I wanted to learn more about these men.

DESPERATE FOR THE WORD

The translator arrived and I began to my left side, having them introduce themselves. Some of these men were quite small in stature, with their feet dangling from the benches on which they were sitting. This first man captured my attention, because he pulled his shirt up to show me where he had been mauled by a tiger. We were on the edge of the jungle. One other man in the group had been mauled by a tiger as well.

But about halfway around the circle, a man was introduced. I will never forget the moment. It was a little dark where he was seated, so I do not remember his face. However, I well remember what he said. He gave his name and then said, "I am eighty years old and I walked for twenty-one days to get here. I do not want to see this conference end."

He wanted more, so much more of the Word and the Spirit whose presence he had felt in that place. I wanted to give him more. I thought to myself, we have pastors' and wives' conferences all over America. There is hardly a week that goes by that someone, somewhere, is not having a conference on how to be successful or how to build a mega-church. But these men are desperate for the Word. Who is going to encourage and feed them? This was probably the incident that led to the conception of our Shepherds' Support Inc. ministry and the latest chapter of Connie's and my life.

Another poignant moment came the following day when we were all back at the house where the former governor (a strong Christian) was hosting us. We saw two separate tribal leaders come and disappear into the house. As we were sitting outside at the tables, the head of Frontier Laborers for Christ came out and said something like, "It is unbelievable what is going on in there. These two tribes (the Rawang and Lisu) have not come together before and cooperated, but are now coming together and, Pastor Troxel, they wanted you to know that they have heard your challenge and accepted it. They will take the Gospel to the surrounding villages which have yet to hear."

Obedience to our Lord's great commission is of the utmost importance. Consider the words of Jesus at the end of his Sermon on the Mount:

> Therefore whoever hears these sayings of Mine, and does them, I will liken him to a wise man who built his house on the rock: and the rain descended, the floods came, and the winds blew and beat on that house; and it did not fall, for it was founded on the rock. But everyone who hears these sayings of Mine, and does not do them, will be like a foolish man who built his house on the sand: and the rain descended, the floods came, and the winds blew and beat on that house; and it fell. And great was its fall.
>
> Matthew 7:24–27 (NKJV)

The only difference between the wise and the foolish was not in what they heard but rather in how they responded.

That unknown eighty-year-old pastor and the leaders of the two different tribes challenged and encouraged me with their thinking. I must keep on running until my race is finished.

"Reaching Out Together"

Reaching out together, God's message the Body heeds;
Together finding where people hurt,
Together meeting their needs.

Together touching each other's lives,
showing the love of Christ;
Together caring, together sharing, and together paying the price.

Reaching out together, declaring the love of God's son,
By reaching down and meeting needs
and moving together as one.

Beloved, let's go together, touching lives day by day.
The Body of Christ, together—Giving itself away![33]

CHAPTER TWELVE

GIVING HIM ALL YOU HAVE...

HEARING HIS CALL

Romans 12 got me started running (spiritually speaking), and it has kept me running all of these years. Let me take you back in time to when I was still a boy. I had trusted Christ as my Savior when I was six or maybe seven, but it wasn't until age fourteen that I was impacted in a transforming kind of way by God's Word. My dad was a dairy farmer. But he was a spiritual man who wanted us to have experiences such as a week at camp or the Youth for Christ Convention, held annually in Winona Lake, Indiana. It was in 1957, at the age of fourteen, that I took another week away from the grind of working in the fields, baling hay, cultivating corn, and numerous other summer duties to attend this annual convention. Estimates stated that as many as 10,000 teenagers gathered from all over the U.S. and Canada to hear gifted musicians and powerful speakers. Dr. Bob Pierce, founder and president of World Vision, was one of the guest speakers on the program that year.

I don't remember much about him or even much of

what he said, (fourteen-year-olds are kind of like that), but I do remember his text. It was Romans 12:1–2. God really came through the text that night. It was as though he was speaking to me. At the invitation, I could not resist walking down that long sawdust trail at the Billy Sunday tabernacle, which since has been demolished. I was positioned close to the back. I gripped the pew in front of me during the invitation song and agonized before making that long walk. But the Spirit won out. I can still remember the feeling that overwhelmed me when I "presented myself" to Him. I felt so fresh and free and new. I found out that the feeling doesn't last forever, but it was long enough to still be fresh in my memory.

When the week was finished, I went back to my routine, but life seemed anything but routine for the next several weeks. My dad had me out cultivating corn in the middle of July. I was on an old tractor with two rows of cultivators just below me. As I watched those ears of corn, one by one, going through the cultivators, I began to see what a waste it was for me to spend the rest of my life cultivating corn, only to see it plowed back underground after the corn was harvested in late fall. Then I began to see people, and the words of Jesus in John 4, regarding the harvest being great, and the sowing and the reaping and the rewards that would follow for both, became very vivid to me.

My dad just happened to be driving by when I reached the end of the field. He was waiting at the fence. He was always checking on us to see how it was going. As I drew closer to him he could see tears in my eyes. He asked me what was wrong. I shared with him my feelings and how I was sensing that maybe God was calling me into some kind of ministry. It was one of those defining moments for me when my dad responded, "Steve, if God is calling you to preach, don't you stoop to be president." I am not sure where he heard it, but I know where I heard it, and it defined the future for me.

CONSIDER ALL THAT HE HAS DONE FOR US

It all began in my life through Romans 12:1–2. Everything in these two verses is predicated upon all that has been written in the first eleven chapters. The connecting word again is "therefore." Paul gives us this wonderful portrait of a God who has created all things, a vivid picture of the awfulness of man's sin, the greatness of our Redeemer, the incredible benefits of our redemption, the Holy Spirit as our guide, the temporary rejection of Israel and their future acceptance of the Gospel. Then he summarizes his thoughts with the great mystery that surrounds God's wisdom and knowledge at the end of chapter 11. And finally the question "How can we ever thank him?" comes to mind.

I don't know about you, but in the ministry we have had so many do so much for us over the years that there is no way that we can adequately thank them. Words just don't seem to be enough. But sometimes words are about the only means we have of expressing our gratitude to those who have so much. They really don't need or want anything else—just our gratefulness.

Think of the incredible wealth and resources of our God. There is nothing that we can give to Him that He doesn't already possess. Romans 11:33 reads in the New Living Translation, "For everything comes from him; everything exists by his power and is intended for his glory."

How can we say thanks to God for all that He has done for us? Paul says that there is one thing we can do. There is only one proper response to such greatness. The best way to give thanks is to present our bodies to Him. Again, Peterson's The Message gets to the heart of the matter:

> So here's what I want you to do, God helping you: take your everyday, ordinary life—your sleeping, eating, going-to-work, and walking-around life—and place it before God as an offering.

Embracing what God does for you is the best thing you can do for him. Don't become so well-adjusted to your culture that you fit into it without even thinking. Instead, fix your attention on God. You'll be changed from the inside out. Readily recognize what he wants from you, and quickly respond to it. Unlike the culture around you, always dragging you down in its level of immaturity, God brings the best out of you, develops well-formed maturity in you.

Romans 12:1–2 (MSG)

There are two central ideas here in the text, both in the form of commands. First, present your body to Him. And second, let Him transform your mind. It sounds simple and logical to me. How about you?

AN APPROPRIATE RESPONSE TO HIM

First, present your body to Him. The word "present," as we saw in Romans 6, is a once and for all presentation. As in marriage, it is a once and for all commitment. But it is also a daily commitment. It was used in a military context. Over the years, as plane-loads of GI's have left for war zones where there is heavy conflict and the very real possibility that they might come home in a body bag, I have wondered how each of them has felt. Certainly they were feeling fear and loneliness and any other number of emotions. But were they thinking, Ah, yes, this is what I signed up for, or were they thinking, Man, I had no idea when I signed up that it was for this?

One thing that each one knows is that the moment they signed their lives on the dotted line they were no longer the ones in control of their lives from that moment onward.

The Greek word here for present is "paristimi." It was also a technical term for "presenting a sacrifice, to place beside for an offering."[34]

There is the old story about three pastors who got together for coffee one morning. Much to their surprise, they discovered that all of their churches had problems with bats infesting their belfries. The bats were making a terrible mess. "I got so mad," the first pastor said, "that I took a shotgun and fired at them. It made holes in the ceiling, but did nothing to the bats."

"I tried trapping them alive," said the second pastor. "Then I drove fifty miles before releasing them, but they beat me back to the church."

The third pastor said, "I haven't had any more problems." They asked him what he did to get rid of them. He said, "I simply baptized and confirmed them and brought them into the church membership. And I haven't seen them since."

We are so prone to commit ourselves to something

or present ourselves to something or maybe even someone, and then just disappear. We take back the commitment and then go on as though nothing happened.

A popular American poster in the past depicted Uncle Sam pointing his finger straight at us. Beneath was the caption, "Uncle Sam wants you!"

I am not comparing Uncle Sam with God. Heaven forbid! But God wants us. He wants our bodies and our minds. Why the bodies? The body is the instrument through which we serve Him. When someone says to me, "I was there in spirit," or "I will be with you in spirit," it doesn't mean anything. Just think, if you are about to get married and invite 500 people to your wedding and everyone of them RSVP's that they cannot make it, but that they "will be with you in spirit," how is that going to make you feel? It doesn't mean a thing.

I think of the old story about the chicken and pig. The chicken said to the pig that it would be nice if they provided the farmer and his wife a nice breakfast of ham and eggs. The pig answered, "For you it is no sacrifice, but for me it represents total commitment." That's it! That's what God wants from us. He is worthy of nothing less. This is the logic of Paul's argument.

Our bodies belong to Him. He fashioned them. He has claimed them for His own. In I Corinthians, Paul asks the question, "Do you not know that your bodies are temples of the Holy Spirit who is in you, whom you have from God, and you are not your own? For you were bought at a price; therefore glorify God in your body and in your spirit, which are God's" (I Corinthians 6:19–20, NKJV).

What would you think if I were to confiscate your keys and claim your house as mine? Then I began to move in and to occupy each of your rooms. I fill them with my own furniture. I make myself at home. You would take me to court or to a mental hospital. Such logic is irrational. Isn't that what Paul is saying here? Anything less than this is irrational and unreasonable.

I heard the story of a woman who had finished shopping and returned to her car. She found four men inside the car. She dropped her shopping bags, drew a handgun, and screamed, "I have a gun, and I know how to use it! Get out of the car." Those men did not wait for a second invitation as they jumped out and ran like crazy.

The woman, somewhat shaken, loaded her shopping bags and then got into the car. But no matter how hard she tried, she could not get her key into the ignition. Then it dawned on her; her car was parked four or five spaces away! She loaded her grocery bags into her own car and then drove to the police station to turn herself in. The desk sergeant to whom she told the story nearly fell off his chair laughing. He pointed to the other end of the counter, where four men were reporting a carjacking by an old woman with thick glasses and curly white hair, less than five feet tall, and carrying a large handgun. No charges were filed.

She thought it was her car, but it really belonged to someone else.

We can hijack our own bodies. They don't belong to us. They belong to God.

God says, "I made you, I purchased you, and now I want to live in you." That sounds reasonable to me. The New Living Translation reads, "I plead with you to give your bodies to God. Let them be a living and holy sacrifice—the kind he will accept" (Romans 12:1–2). When you think of what He has done for you, is this too much to ask? Good question!

God has no physical body. This is why He desires your body to serve Him. Your heart becomes His heart to show compassion to others. Your hands become His hands to touch others. Your feet become His feet to take the gospel to others. Each member of your body now belongs to Him. This is your reasonable act of worship.

THE BATTLE IS IN THE MIND

We must also present our minds to Him (Romans 12:2).

The mind and body go together. The Phillips version on this verse is so familiar that many of you know it by heart: "Don't let the world squeeze you into its own mold, but let God remold your minds from within, so that you may prove in practice that the plan of God for you is good, meets all his demands and moves toward the goal of true maturity."

There are two words that stand out here. First is the word "mold." Back on the farm we went through a period of time where we put water tanks out in the field for our dairy cows. We had molds that we would form and then we would pour cement into those molds. The cement would conform to the image of the mold.

We get our English word "scheme" from this Greek word. The devil is behind all of the scheming around us. He uses the world and the flesh to bring us down and take us out of the race. In fact, the only other time this word is used is in I Peter 1:14 where Peter is encouraging his readers to go on and pursue living by the Spirit. He writes, "Obey God because you are his children. Don't slip back into ways of doing evil; you didn't know any better then" (NLT). That idea behind the two words "slip back" is to say, "Don't let the world squeeze you back into its mold." There is this never-ending pressure to conform to this world.

Satan is "like a roaring lion, walking about seeking

whom he may devour" (I Peter 5:8, NKJV). As a kid, my favorite cartoon series was the roadrunner and the coyote. The coyote was forever conniving how he might trap the roadrunner. His plans always ended in futility. Unfortunately, our enemy is far more successful in his deceitful scheming.

For example, the world is forever bombarding us with false messages. It is all based upon an erroneous set of values, such as your self-worth is based upon how beautiful you are or how athletic you are or how much money you make or where you live or the kind of clothes you wear or the perfume you buy. If we are not careful, we can buy into all of the world's lies. We get caught up in living for the wrong things and waste our lives.

As Paul describes the armor that we must put on in Ephesians 6:10–20, he mentions faith in verse 16: "Above all taking the shield of faith with which you will be able to quench all the fiery darts [flaming missiles] of the wicked one" (NKJV).

The whole purpose of the car bombings and rocket launchers and other forms of weaponry used by the terrorists today is to destroy and demoralize the peoples that are targeted. Satan's methodology is the same. He is on a "seek and destroy" mission.

How can we defeat him? First of all, we must have

a wartime mentality. We have been lulled into this false sense of peace. Second, we must guard what we allow to come into our minds. We are often much more selective about what we allow to come into our mouths than what we allow into our minds. Yet the food passes through the body in a short period of time. But what we allow into our minds lingers indefinitely. It fashions and molds us in ways that we do not understand.

One of the great hindrances to spiritual growth today is the internet and TV. While there is much good that can benefit one, there is also much evil that can defeat one. This is to say nothing of the time that is wasted. As Christians, we are to be "redeeming the time because the days are evil" (Ephesians 5:15, NKJV). Pornography might well be the greatest curse on men's minds today. It controls and weakens and cuts off our spiritual power.

We have a transformer between our neighbor's house and ours, and it has malfunctioned several times over the years we have lived here. It usually occurs in the middle of the night. When it happens, there is no power. There are no lights, air conditioning, refrigeration, or anything else depending on electricity. It is a helpless feeling. Why? We are cut off from the power source. This is the result of pornography in our churches today. We have no power. The enemy is having a field day. Where is the answer?

Paul gives us the answer right here: "Don't be conformed, but rather be transformed by the renewing of your mind." The word "transformed" comes from the Greek word that gives us our English word "metamorphosis." This word is used sparingly in the New Testament. It was used of Jesus at His transfiguration. He was transformed before their very eyes. Of course, when we think of this process of metamorphosis, we think of the lowly caterpillar. It is an ugly little worm that is so earthbound that it crawls on the ground. But one day soon it will be a beautiful butterfly unlimited in its mobility.

In II Corinthians 3:18, Paul uses the word to describe the change that is taking place in each one of us as we are beholding Christ: "But we all, with unveiled face, beholding as in a mirror the glory of the Lord, are being transformed into the same image from glory to glory, just as by the Spirit of the Lord" (NKJV).

By beholding Him and becoming intimate with Him, we become like Him. As we feed on His Word and allow Him to speak to us, we become like Him. My wife and I married back in 1962. We are amazed at how much we have become one in terms of our likes and dislikes. We can almost finish each other's sentences. We have, in that sense, become like one another through intimacy in relationship. I have taken on the likeness of my dad. Why shouldn't I? He had a profound impact on my development in those early years. We take on the likeness of those we spend time with, whether for good or for bad. This is why the Proverbs warn us about the kind of friends we keep.

This is how we renew the mind, through the lifelong pursuit of intimacy with our Creator. As the New Living Translation reminds us, "then you will know what God wants you to do, and you will know how good and pleasing and perfect his will really is" (Romans 12:2). As I look back over my life, I can trace nearly every blessed experience back to that defining moment as a fourteen-year-old boy. Had I pursued my own course and tried to hold on to my life, I would have (in the words of Jesus, "lost it") missed out on so much. We have met so many wonderful people, ministered in faraway places to audiences large and small, and seen so much of God's beautiful creation that if I tried to describe them to you, it would take many books. All of this traced back to that decisive moment in my life when I said, "I belong to you, Lord Jesus. What there is of me, you can have it."

ALLOWING HIM TO POSSESS US

Years ago, in the south of Europe one morning, a tall, slender, boyish-faced fellow, with a Jewish cast of feature, entered one of the old cathedrals. The cathedral was famous for its organ, and was yet more famous for the organist who brought the music from its pipes. But the years had gone and the strength had gone, and a young man was appointed to do the heavy work, while the old man was appointed the custodian of the keys. And he spent most of his waking hours in the cathedral with the old organ that he loved as a mother loves her babe.

The young fellow who entered the cathedral that morning seemed to know the story. He sought out the old man, and said, "I hear you have a wonderful organ here." That was enough: the old man's eyes danced and gleamed.

"It's the finest in the fatherland," he said.

"I have heard so," said the young fellow, "and I thought I would like to try it. Will you loan me the key?" And the old man drew himself back.

"I could not do that," he said, with continental politeness. "You will pardon me, sir, but you know it is a very wonderful organ, and we are very careful who touches it; I could not give you the keys."

But the young fellow persisted. He said, "I love music. I have traveled a good many miles to see this organ of yours; I play a little. Please loan me the key." So he persisted, and persistence always wins.

There are no exceptions to that law. And by and by, he had the key and opened the manual, and drew out some stops, and turned on the power while the old man stood back there against the pillar, wondering how that key got out of his fingers.

Then the music began, and he forgot everything else. He found himself saying, "I thought I knew all the music our organ had in it. I did not know it had such exquisite music in it as this man is bringing out. Who can he be?" And he stood spellbound, with his eyes big, listening. The music began very softly, just like the sighing of the zephyr breeze in the tree tops, then it rose up and rolled out. Then the storm broke, the thunder roared, and the lightning nearly blinded him, the old man. And the rain? He was wet. It was all so real to him. Then the storm passed, and birds were singing. Then the music grew soft, just like a baby breathing in its sleep in its mother's arms. At last the music stopped, and the young fellow locked up the organ, and brought back the key, and said, "Thank you. It is a wonderful organ. I am very grateful to you."

But the old man, not taking the key, said, "Who are you? What is your name?"

And the young fellow modestly dropped his eyes and said, "My name is Felix Mendelssohn, sir."

And the old man's eyes filled up, and he said, "To think—the master was here and I refused him the keys."[35]

The Master is here. And He asks for the keys to you. You will never regret turning those keys over to Him.

Back on the farm, we had an expression that we frequently heard in one form or another. It is this: "you must drive a stake into the ground." It comes from building a fence around a field. When we would get to the end of the field and we were about to turn in a different direction, we would drive a stake into the ground to anchor the corner post. We would then use some number nine wire to secure the fence post to the stake in the ground. This would give the necessary support for both lines of the fence.

Driving a stake in the ground becomes a turning point in your life. This is what I did back in 1957. This is what you can do right now. Let this become the moment that you turn from your sin (repentance—self control) and turn to Christ (faith—His control) and give it all to Him. You will be amazed at what He can do with your life that you never could do on your own.

This moment will keep you running right into eternity.

> O Lord, I give myself to thee and all that I possess. I
> lay aside my sinful self, and claim thy righteousness.
> My will lies shattered at thy feet; I pray

thy will be done. My only plea to live
for thee and magnify thy Son.

O humbly may I serve thee, Lord, as in
thy will I tread. And may I live anew
in Christ, as risen from the dead.
Then closely walking by thy side, may love
flow out through me, that those whom thou
shalt lead my way, may too find life in thee.

Chorus: May Christ be seen in me, O
Lord. Hear thou, my earnest plea.
O take me, fill me, use me, Lord,
till Christ be seen in me.[36]

CHAPTER THIRTEEN

MEET A FORGIVING TRANSLATOR IN ROMANIA

PSALM 40 TO MY RESCUE

I mentioned earlier that I had gone through burnout back in 1997. I lost my passion for God and people. I was simply going through the motions of ministry and did not know where to go for help. Help often comes from the most unlikely sources. This time it was a translator in Romania who was there for me, and he encouraged me to keep on running. He shall remain anonymous.

But before I get to him, let me tell you a little more about where I was. In Psalm 40:1–5, the psalmist found himself in a horrible pit. It was a deep roaring chasm. It was a noisy place where he felt disoriented. It was a lonely place. When you are in it, you feel cut off from the people around you. No one understands. No one seems to care. Some might not even recognize that you are in the pit. Pits cause you to disappear. You are below the radar screen. You are stuck down in the miry clay. The picture is of one who could not find his foothold, but slips and sinks further and further into the darkness and abyss. Have you ever been there? Perhaps you are there right now as you are reading this. My prayer is that my story might give you hope.

Here I was in this condition, with Connie and me leaving our daughter, her husband, and four grandchildren in Italy and heading off to Romania, where I was to be the featured speaker for 1,200 pastors and missionaries at the Romanian Baptist Conference. We linked up with missionaries in Zurich, Switzerland, who because of their present ministry need to remain anonymous. After vacationing for several days in that area, we began our drive eastward toward Romania. It seemed that the farther eastward we went, the more oppression I felt because of the depressing circumstances. We went down through Austria, on to Hungary, on through Transylvania, and through most of Romania until we arrived in Bucharest. For us, it was a journey into the past, when life was far simpler. Horse and ox-drawn carts were common place out on the roads and in the fields. God knew that I needed this time for healing.

However, at that time, because of the rainy, cold, dreary weather conditions, Bucharest seemed to be a pit in itself. We were staying in an apartment above a storefront on a very busy street corner where the electric trolley cars came by every few minutes and literally caused the apartment to shake. Yes, it was a noisy pit.

The only time when they ceased operating was between 2:00 and 4:00 in the morning.

It was also too dangerous for me to do my usual running. This had been my means of releasing tension and dealing with stress since 1975. The reason for not running seems strange. Packs of wild dogs roamed the streets back then and still do to this day. At that time, the Romanians estimated 600,000 wild dogs were in Bucharest alone. The dogs also, along with the people, were the victims of the oppressive reign of Nicolae Ceausescu, the madman who caused so much suffering during the latter years of communism in that country. Before the revolution in December of 1989, he tried to collect the people, taking them off their farms and their private dwellings and putting them in these masses of high-rise, inefficient, and dark apartments. They were not permitted to take their dogs with them. The dogs were left to fend for themselves. Walking would not make them curious, but running does. I found out that running was not a wise thing to do during our two weeks of ministry there. Consequently, I thought that this would be two of the longest weeks of my life.

HOSPITALITY IN ROMANIA

During the first several days with our (wonderful host and hostess), I had time to read some good books on

Romania, its people and history. It would help me to better relate to these Christian leaders to whom I would be ministering. And somehow, as I read these secular books, I was able to get a better grasp on what I was going through personally. It gave me a different perspective. God took the focus away from me. He gave me a burden for the people of Romania and Hungary. My passion was beginning to return. I would need this passion the very next week.

We took a train from Bucharest to Braila, about a three-hour ride. Two other couples from Wayside Chapel joined us for the ride: Acie and Marilyn Johnson and Lannie and Melba Green. Upon arrival in Braila, Connie and I stayed with the pastor and his wife. We had no heat and, most of the time, no hot water. There were times when we were without water altogether. One morning, as Connie and I were lying in bed together trying to keep warm, I said to her, "You know, dear, we are going to have to make some changes in our lives when we get back to the States. The first change that we must make is that we will need to start bathing again."

In spite of these inconveniences, the pastor and his wife were so warm in the hospitality department that it made up for the lack of warmth in other areas. They did not have a lot of anything at that time in Romania in the way of conveniences. One day I asked Pastor Joseph out of curiosity, "How many people are in your congregation?" He said, "About 500." I asked him how many of them had cars. He thought for a moment and said, "Ten." Then he added with a twinkle in his eye, "Only six of them work." I made a mental note to kiss my 1984 Mazda pickup (which was nothing more than a motorcycle wrapped in tin foil) when I returned back to San Antonio.

This is when we met Maria (chapter 1). Maria assured us of her prayers as we were leaving Braila and beginning a twelve-hour ride by car to Cluj, in the western part of Romania. When we arrived at the conference, we felt as though we were being a bit stiff-armed by the leadership. Pastor Joseph was a leading pastor among the Baptists there. And because of our investment in his home church, he influenced the leadership to invite me to be their keynote speaker for the conference. But they knew nothing about me, and it appeared to us that they were wondering why we were asked to come and be the featured speakers. Connie was singing for the conference.

As I was about to address the conference for the first time, we had another one of those moments that is forever in my memory. It is as though that time is frozen in my memory bank. Connie was singing behind this huge pulpit. Seven or so of us men were sitting just behind Connie, somewhat concealed by the sheer size of the pulpit. My translator, whom I had not met until that moment, was a gifted translator. He had translated for Billy Graham when Billy had been there before the fall of communism. As Connie began to sing, my translator turned to me and said, "What are you going to speak on?" That is a fair question for a translator at this moment. I shared how I was going to speak on the three great motivations for missions found in Acts 1:1–11. First would be the resurrection of Christ. "He proved Himself to be alive after His suffering by many infallible proofs, being seen by them during forty days and speaking of the things pertaining to the kingdom of God" (Acts 1:1–3, NKJV). Second would be the sending of His Holy Spirit. The Spirit would come and "you shall receive power when the Holy Spirit has come upon you; and you shall be witnesses to Me in Jerusalem, and in all Judea and Samaria, and to the end of the earth" (Acts 1:8–11, NKJV). And finally would be the second coming of Christ.

As He was taken up from them and the disciples were gazing up into the heavens, two angels stood by them who also said, "Men of Galilee, why do you stand gazing up into heaven? This same Jesus, who

was taken up from you into heaven, will so come in
like manner as you saw Him go into heaven."

Acts 1:9–11 (NKJV)

By the time I had given him this synopsis of my
message, Connie was nearing the end of her song. He
then said to me, "Now listen, don't underestimate the
intelligence and spiritual depth of these men. They are
well-read and well-grounded in the Word. These people know what it is to suffer for their faith. Too many
speakers come in from the West and preach on John
3:16 and tell them that God loves them. These men
know that already. They need more than that. They
need meat and not milk."

Any of you who have spoken to large groups know
how devastating a moment and a thought like this can
be. This was not what I needed to bring me out of
the pit. I thought, Do I have meat, or do I only bring
them milk? Then I sent up an arrow prayer. "Lord, you
turned the water into wine in Cana of Galilee. If this is
milk, please, now, turn it into meat."

A RENEWED PASSION

Both of us stood to the pulpit, and I immediately started
out with a joke (I couldn't break with tradition even in
a foreign country). A man was walking around in a pet

store one day when all at once he heard this squeaky voice on the other side of the room. "Hey you!" (I did it in high falsetto and, amazingly, my translator followed suit). The man said, "Who, me?" The bird said, "Yea, you, come on over here." The man did as the bird told him. He looked down into the cage and said, "What do you want?" The bird looked intently at him and said, "You're ugly."

The man was taken aback by the bird's analysis of his physical attractiveness, but the man proceeded to walk around the store. The same thing happened again. (I will spare taking you through it.) It then happened again and again until the man's self image was nearly crushed. He could stand it no longer. He went to the proprietor of the store and asked him if he had heard what his bird was saying to him. The man assured him that he did hear the bird. He came around the counter, went over to the bird cage, opened the door, grabbed the bird, pulled him out, and slapped him along the head several times and said, "Now don't you ever say anything like that ever again to any of my customers."

A few minutes later the customer is walking around the store again when the same high- pitched, squeaky voice is heard from the other side of the room. You remember the scenario: "Hey, you." "Who, me?" "Yea, you, come on over here." He does as requested, and looks down into the beady little eyes of the bird and says, "Yea, what do you want?" The bird hesitated for a moment and then said, "You know!"

The place was already fully engaged as they listened carefully to the translation. When the punch line was given the church erupted with laughter. I sensed that I had them with me from that moment on. I then said, "I am not going to tell you anything that you do not already know. I only want to bring to your remembrance and encourage you by the things that we already know."

For one entire hour I sensed God's Spirit speaking powerfully through me. When I finally brought it to a conclusion, my translator turned to me in front of everyone and embraced me and said, "Please forgive me. Please forgive me!" Of course I forgave him. The moderator came to the pulpit and asked the crowd to divide up in small groups and pray and recommit themselves to the great historical truths of which they had just been reminded.

The best news for me was that I was back. I was out of the pit. Maybe I wasn't washed up yet. Maybe God could still use me. A year later, back in San Antonio, I received a phone call. It came from the same translator. I told him that my time in Romania was a turning point in my life and ministry. I shared how I had thought that I was finished, all washed-up. He said, "Now why would you think something like that?" I thought to myself, I don't know. Why did I? Time does change things.

The Keswick Convention (established to proclaim the life of Christ in relation to each believer) in 1931 included a message on Psalm 40 by A. Lindsay Glegg. He has a five-fold outline on the chapter:

1. Brought up! "Out of a horrible pit, out of the miry clay."
2. Set up! "He set my feet upon a rock."
3. Held up! "He established my steps."
4. Tuned up! "He has put a new song in my mouth, praise to our God…"
5. Caught up! "You are my help and my deliverer. Do not delay, O my God." He takes this verse out of context by his own admission and applies this to the day when we are taken up in to glory.[37]

Now I can say that I remember in my running when I fell into a horrible pit from which I could not get out. God used this translator and these Romanian pastors and missionaries to encourage me to get up and to keep on running. My thanks are extended to each one of you. I am still running today because of men and women like you.

He took my feet from the miry clay,
yes he did, and yes he did,
And placed them on that rock to
stay, yes he did, yes he did.

I can tell the world about this, I can
tell the nations I'm blessed,
Tell them that Jesus made me whole, and
he brought joy, joy to my soul.[38]

CHAPTER FOURTEEN
ABIDING IN CHRIST
JOHN 15

In a trial in a small town, a prosecuting attorney called his first witness to the stand: an elderly grandmother.

He approached her and asked, "Mrs. Jones, do you know me?"

She responded, "Why yes, I do know you, Mr. Williams. I've known you since you were a young boy. And frankly, you've been a big disappointment to me. You lie, you cheat on your wife, and you manipulate people and talk about them behind their backs. You think you're a big shot when you haven't the brains to realize you never will amount to anything more than a two-bit paper pusher. Yes, I know you."

The lawyer was stunned. Not knowing what else to do, he pointed across the room and asked, "Mrs. Jones, do you know the defense attorney?'

She replied, "Why yes, I do. I've known Mr. Bradley since he was a youngster, too. He's lazy, bigoted, and he has a drinking problem. He can't build a normal relationship with anyone and his law practice is one of the worst in the entire state. Not to mention he cheated on his wife with three different women. Yes, I know him."

The defense attorney almost died at this point. The judge brought the courtroom to silence, called both counselors to the bench, and in a very quiet voice said, "If either of you low-lifes asks her if she knows me, you'll be jailed for contempt."

The truth is that apart from Christ, none of us will ever amount to anything that will stand the test of time. We are all sinners and in desperate need of Him for salvation. There is none righteous, no not one (Romans 3:10).

But once we have experienced His redeeming grace, we go on needing His enabling grace and power. We cannot do it on our own. He never designed us to live independently of Him. I shudder when I think of how much of my ministry has been done in my own strength, depending upon my own abilities.

TRYING TO LIVE LIFE WITHOUT HIM

A couple of years ago, at Christmas time, we had a knock on our front door. I answered and discovered that the caregiver for my next-door-neighbor, now over one hundred years of age, needed my help to transfer my neighbor from her wheel chair to her big soft chair. She had been hospitalized earlier in the week and was experiencing something of a semi-conscious state of mind, not fully aware that I was even there. Her caregiver informed me that she, herself, had a bad back and could not help me. I saw that as no problem. I was a big, strong farm boy, as I remembered myself to be. I knew what it was to throw around sixty to seventy-five pounds of baled hay (forty-five years ago). I can do this, I thought to myself. I didn't need any help. I put one arm under her legs, another behind her back and began to lift her, instructing her caregiver to pull the wheel chair out from under her. She folded up like an accordion, giving no resistance. Her forehead was now smashed against her knees. I was tenuously balancing her on my knees. I was in deep trouble. I was about to lose her. Gravity pull was winning. The caregiver (a small-framed Hispanic Catholic lady) was cheering me on with the audible prayer, "Jesus, help him. Help him, Jesus!" Finally, when I was exhausted, I began to say, "Jesus, I really do need your help. And if you will help me I promise to never do this again." Somehow we managed to get her maneuvered into her big soft chair. I breathed a big sigh of relief and wrote that down as one of those things that I would never, ever do again.

How much of what you are doing is being done in dependence upon Him? All through John's Gospel, John is writing to prove that Jesus is the Son of God. John follows Jesus carefully and, more than the other

Gospels, shows us how Jesus modeled total dependency upon the Father.

In John 5:19, "Then Jesus answered and said to them, 'Most assuredly, I say to you, the Son can do nothing of Himself, but what He sees the Father do; for whatever He does, the Son also does in like manner'" (NKJV).

In John 5:30, he said, "I can of Myself do nothing" (NKJV).

Even prior to His raising of Lazarus in John 11:41, He lifted up His eyes and said, "Father, I thank You that You have heard Me. And I know that You always hear Me, but because of the people who are standing by I said this, that they may believe that You sent Me" (NKJV).

He was simply showing to others that He was not acting on His own, not independent of the Father.

And now in John 15, as He is preparing His disciples for His departure, He wants them to come to the same understanding, that without Him they could do nothing (verse 5).

This teaching was also a turning point in these last words of Jesus, commonly known as the Upper Room Discourse. According to John 14:31, they were leaving the upper room. He invited them to follow Him. He wound His way from the western side of the old city, and down across the Tyropeon Valley, which separated the Temple from the rest of the city, around the wall, skirting the Temple area, down into the Kidron Valley, across the brook, and then up the slope of the Mount of Olives.

There were vineyards terraced around the hillsides of the old city. He might have even stopped in one of them and pointed out the grapes, the branches, and the vines. Of course, today, vineyards are even commonplace in many parts of our own country. And still today there is no lack of vineyards in Israel. They dot the landscape in many parts of that tiny country.

It could be that they might have been positioned to be able to see the great golden vine, the national symbol of Israel, perched high on the front of the temple. Even today, a clump of grapes from the vine is a symbol of national identity seen in Israel.

That symbolism took them back to numerous Old Testament passages such as Psalm 80:8–9. We read the words of Asaph: "You have brought a vine out of Egypt; You have cast out the nations and planted it. You prepared room for it and caused it to take deep root, and it filled the land" (NKJV).

Or in Isaiah, where Israel is spoken of as the beloved vineyard of God:

My well-beloved has a vineyard, on a very fruit-

ful hill. He dug it up and cleared out its stones,
and planted it with the choicest vine. He built a
tower in its midst, and also made a winepress in it;
so He expected it to bring forth good grapes, but it
brought forth wild grapes.

Isaiah 5:1–2 (NKJV)

Because of this, God said, regarding Israel, "I will
take away its hedge, and it shall be burned; and break
down its wall, and it shall be trampled down. I will lay
it waste" (Isaiah 5:5–6, NKJV). Of course, history proves
this prophecy to have been true.

Now we know that God is not finished with Israel
yet. His plans for them will yet be fulfilled. At the end
of the seven years of tribulation there will be a recogni-
tion of the Messiah and a national day of repentance.
Zechariah 12:10 reads, "And I will pour on the house of
David and on the inhabitants of Jerusalem the Spirit
of grace and supplication: then they will look on Me
whom they pierced. Yes, they will mourn for Him as
one mourns for his only son, and grieve for Him as one
grieves for a firstborn" (NKJV).

Again in Revelation 1:7, we read, "Behold, He is
coming with clouds, and every eye will see Him, even
they who pierced Him. And all the tribes of the earth
will mourn because of Him. Even so, Amen" (NKJV).

With Israel's unbelief and rejection, they were no longer a fruitful vineyard.

JESUS IS THE TRUE VINE, WE ARE THE BRANCHES

Jesus uses the vine metaphor to teach some wonderful spiritual truths about Himself and His followers. He refers to Himself in this way: "I am the True Vine" (John 15:1). This is another one of the seven great "I Am" statements in John's Gospel. Jesus is the true vine. He is the real deal. He is not just a mere copy or symbol of something, as Israel was. Israel was only an imitation or type of the true Vine. Jesus is the original, the one and only. All life is in Him.

All of this is so critical and basic to our understanding of the Christian life. He is the Vine, we are the branches. It is His life that is to reside in us and flow through us, and the end result is fruit. This is the natural process.

Do not miss the Father in the metaphor. He is the vinedresser, or the caretaker. He takes good care of the Vine, His Son. The Father also gives tender care to the branches. He wants to see fruit.

Notice several key words in this metaphor:

First is the word "branch" (John 15:2). He takes away every branch that does not bear fruit. I don't know what the wording is in your translation, but some include a side note with the rendering, "He lifts up." Many translators have missed the basic meaning of this Greek word "airo." It can be translated as "takes away" or "cuts off" or as "lifts up." In this context it seems more appropriate to render it "lifts up." This is precisely what the vinedresser will do. He lifts up the unproductive branches out of the mud and dirt, cleans them off and brings them to new productivity. There are many fruits and vegetables that do not do well when they are lying on the ground. Grapes are one of them. They do best up away from the ground, hanging freely in the air.

I remember the first time that this came to life for me was in 1978, when a group of us were taken on a five-week tour of Israel by Dr. Arnold Fruchtenbaum. This was our first time in Israel. Since then, we have taken numerous groups and have made the same observation. At one point we stopped along the road and Arnold showed us a vine with the branches. Some of the tendrils were propped up from the ground. They were supported by wires and poles. This is in order that they might become more fruitful. They are more exposed to the sun. They are drawn closer to the vinedresser. God uses circumstances in our lives and creates inner desires to move us closer to Him. And the whole purpose is that we might become more fruitful.

There is a second part of the process mentioned here in verse 2. Our translations use the word "prunes." It comes from the Greek word "katharizo." We get our English word "catharsis" from this word. It means to cleanse or purge. The vinedresser strips away all that is harmful: the insects, the dead growth, and whatever else is collecting on the vine and harming the branches.

Maybe you are undergoing the stripping process right now in your life. You might have been stripped of your job, a relationship, a part of your income, your health, or even your ministry. Why does He allow this? The purpose is to draw our hearts to Him, so that we might find our life and significance in Him alone.

Next, we have the word "fruit." We have "fruit," "more fruit" (verse 2), and "much fruit" (verse 5). What is the fruit? What does that look like in our lives? I used to think that it was strictly winning others to Christ. That is important and an essential focus of our mission. But I think that the fruit referred to here must be the fruit of the Spirit, mentioned in Galatians 5.

> But the fruit of the [Holy] Spirit [the work which His presence within accomplishes] is love, joy [gladness], peace, patience [an even temper, for-bearance], kindness, goodness [benevolence], faith-fulness [meekness, humility], gentleness, self-con-

trol [self-restraint, continence]. Against such things there is no law [that can bring a charge].

Galatians 5:22–23 (AMP)

How does your character measure up against this list, coming from His Spirit dwelling within us?

HE WANTS US TO BEAR FRUIT

His Word is the key in this whole process of fruit producing. We cannot expect to bear this kind of fruit apart from the cleansing agent of the Word. This is the instrument that the Holy Spirit uses in our lives. It was the agent that Jesus used to set His own disciples apart. One of the first passages that I learned as a teenager was Psalm 119:9–11: "How can a young person stay pure [cleanse his way]? By obeying your word and following its rules. I have tried my best to find you—don't let me wander from your commands. I have hidden your word in my heart that I might not sin against you" (NLT).

God reminded Joshua in Joshua 1:8–9, "Study this Book of the law continually. Meditate on it day and night so you may be sure to obey all that is written in it. Only then will you succeed. I command you—be strong and courageous! Do not be afraid or discouraged. For the Lord your God is with you wherever you go" (NLT).

Oh the joys of those who do not follow the advice of the wicked, or stand around with sinners, or join in with mockers. But they delight in the law of the Lord, meditating on it day and night. They are like trees planted along the riverbank, bearing fruit each season. Their leaves never wither, and they prosper in all they do.

Psalm 1:1–3 (NLT)

Years ago, my father had a large poplar tree on the back of one of his properties. In fact, it was the largest poplar tree in the state of Ohio. It took five grown men standing against the trunk of the tree with arms extended wide to reach around the tree at shoulder height. It stood by itself, buffeted by the winds, with no protection from the other trees. This probably caused its root system to become massive. More importantly, there was a little stream of water that ran right by the tree, which gave it the constant water the tree needed for its growth.

There have been so many times over the years that I have found myself in some deep valleys, feeling overwhelmed in discouragement, absorbed in self-pity. The last thing I wanted to do was to spend time in the Word and prayer. But this is what I needed the most. And preaching weekly gives a structure for discipline in this area. You cannot function effectively in preaching for very long if you are not feasting on His word and responding in prayer and thanksgiving.

A number of years ago, as I began a series through I Peter, I challenged our congregation to memorize the book as I began the series. Two ladies accepted the challenge and, at last count, they had memorized six books together. One of these ladies said to me just weeks before I stepped down from Wayside that she could not put into words what this discipline of memorization had meant to her. Nothing cleanses and prunes us better than the Word. It will hold us up and sustain us and give us hope in the darkest hours of our lives. The reason for this is that this book is truth. In your times of greatest temptation, this Word will keep you from falling if you heed its advice and let it dwell richly in you.

Are you in the midst of a pruning process right now in your life? Is God using the sharp circumstances of life to cut off some old growth that is hindering you? It might be some old ways of thinking, some habits, or some addictions, as He confronts you with the Word of Truth. Even churches go through periods of pruning. During my thirty-four years at Wayside, we experienced the ebb and flow of growth and pruning when it came to numbers of attendees. Pastor, don't get discouraged by what you see. Consider it to be part of His pruning process that there might be even greater growth. Pruning is a necessary thing and a good thing for growth to continue. As you follow the process through there will be fruit, more fruit, and much fruit.

What is our responsibility in all of this?

THE KEY TO FRUIT BEARING IS ABIDING IN HIM

The final word is "abide" (John 15:4–5). Actively, we must abide in Him. Passively, we must allow Him to abide in us. Both relationships are essential.

The idea is that we choose by an act of the will. We must be open to Him and have a heart to respond to His leading. It is essential that we constantly expose ourselves to the light and stay close to Him. That is what it means to abide in Him. This is what Bible study and prayer are all about. When we read His Word, we listen for Him to speak to us. When we pray, we speak to Him. It needs to be an ongoing dialogue, just as you have in any relationship. It cannot be all one-sided. Abiding means to keep the love relationship intimate with Him.

This was the problem with the church at Ephesus in Revelation 2. They were doing many commendable things, just as we might be doing. But the Lord challenged them in verse 4: "Nevertheless I have this against you, that you have left your first love" (NKJV). Love is something that we can choose to do or not to do. We can leave, but not lose our first love. It was the same word used in Matthew 4:20, regarding the disciples: "They [Peter and Andrew his brother] immediately left their nets and followed Him" (NKJV).

When partners begin to stray from one another, they might make reference to the fact that just as they fell into love, they have now fallen out of love, as though they were helpless to do anything about it. That is not biblical love. Love is a choice, an act of the will. We choose to abide in Him. Or we can run the other way and try to make life work without Him. But it cannot work that way. Life was not set up any other way than to work through His abiding presence.

One of my great fears for the church today is that we have become so dependent upon the world's method on how to build a large organization. We have become slick at using technology. We use almost any means to pack them into our churches. We have entertainment that is second to none. We look so successful on the outside. Where are we taking our people? What does the Lord really think? Is it coming from Him? Sometimes I want to ask when in church services, Does Jesus have anything to do with this?

Ray Stedman was the first one whom I ever heard use the glove as an illustration. He would hold up a glove and speak about all of its wonderful qualities, its fine craftsmanship, the materials of which it was made, the form in which it was put together. It was fashioned to fit around a human hand. But that glove by itself could do absolutely nothing. All it could do was lie there and look like a glove. It was helpless. Then he would stick his hand in the glove and watch it come to life. It was full of life and now capable of doing anything that the human hand could do. That is what His life will do in us. Are you presently abiding in Him?

Oh, dear Father, precious Friend; teach me to abide.
Take me in your tender arms, there to safely hide.

Let your heart flow into mine, let my will subside.
May your every joy be mine, teach me to abide.

'Till our hearts but beat as one,
purge me from all pride.
Oh, dear God, I've but one prayer:
teach me to abide.[39]

CHAPTER FIFTEEN

MEET A BANKER, A STEWARDESS, AND AN ENVIRONMENTAL SCIENTIST

The title of my chapter reminds me of the story of the woman who had been married to four different husbands, each in different professions. First she was married to a banker, then an entertainer, followed by a preacher, and finally she ended up with an undertaker. When asked if there was any method to her madness, she responded, "One for the money, two for the show, three to make ready, and four to go."

It is amazing what God uses to keep us running at times when we might be wavering a bit in our commitment to stay in the race. I had an unforgettable commercial airline flight during which I met several people whom I would like to introduce to you in this chapter.

Allow me to set the scene: I was traveling from San Antonio to the Philadelphia area in the fall of 2005 to speak at a missions conference in an old historic church. The flights up and back were quite eventful and full of surprises.

It began in San Antonio. I was traveling alone, as a family matter kept Connie from being able to accompany me.

A HINDU BANKER

Traveling on Southwest Airlines, where there are no assigned seats, I found myself on a very full flight, seated next to the aisle. The man next to me was a small man of Indian descent. He was now a banker up in the New Jersey area. Raul was also Hindu in his faith. I introduced myself to him, and we began a conversation that soon turned to spiritual matters. As I recall, I asked him about India, because at that point we had not been there. Soon we will be going back for our second time. I was interested in finding out more about his homeland and what the people believed. Of course, Hinduism is the prominent religion there. I asked him what he believed as a Hindu. He proceeded to tell me what he knew about his religion. It became quite apparent rather rapidly that he knew very little about the long-held religious beliefs of his ancestors. Two things became quite clear regarding his beliefs. First, Hinduism is a system of works like all other religions. Second, you can never really know for sure anything about the afterlife and where you will ultimately be in eternity.

I started talking with him about the uniqueness of Christ and therefore of the Christian faith. However, our time was short. The pilot was about to land the aircraft in Houston and allow passengers to deplane, if that were their final destination, and allow other passengers to come on board, before continuing the flight to Philadelphia.

I was interested in moving up to a bulkhead seat, and when I mentioned this to Raul, he asked if he might join me. That was a pretty good hint that he was not turned off by my boldness in presenting the Gospel to him. We took our new seats and resumed our conversation.

I continued speaking about the uniqueness of Christ and Christianity. In every other religion, salvation and heaven are based upon what man can do for God and you never know if it is enough. But in Christianity, it is what God has done for us and it is more than enough. It is a finished work.

I spoke of our sin problem and how God Himself provided the answer for sin. He came down to earth and took upon Himself human flesh and blood in order that He might die for us and thereby, once and forever, remove the problem of sin and enable us to have a personal relationship with Him. I showed him several verses in the book of Romans dealing with our sin and where it ultimately leads us. I had him read the verses out loud. It was a long conversation that led us up to this point. He was listening intently and asking good questions. I felt led, by the Spirit, I believe, to take him further and tell him based upon many verses, "Raul, you can trust Christ right now, 36,000 feet up in the air, in this plane. Raul, you can know right now that your sins are forgiven and that when you die you will go to heaven. You can settle that once and for all by trusting Jesus Christ as your Lord and Savior. You can do it right now."

I will never forget that moment. I saw a man struggle as few struggle in their decision. Tears began to form in his eyes and began running down his cheeks. There was a battle that was being waged for his soul. He was, no doubt, considering the cost. This successful banker was in the midst of a life and death struggle.

I waited for his answer. Finally, it came: "Not yet," he could barely get out. I told him that I understood the struggle and I admired his intellectual honesty. I asked if I could pray for him. He nodded affirmatively, not quite sure what I was about to do. He had the look of a man who was about to undergo some life threatening surgery. I prayed, only loud enough for Raul to hear me, I thought, that Jesus Christ would become so real to him that he would hesitate no longer and that all of his concerns would be fully dealt with soon. When I finished praying for him I gave him a copy of Andy Stanley's little book entitled How Good is Good Enough.[40] He assured me that he would read it.

A STEWARDESS UNDER CONVICTION

We were approaching the end of our flight, but final preparations for landing had not taken place yet. I stood to my feet and stretched my legs. As I did so, I heard the voice of the stewardess who asked me if she could talk to me. Pat had been seated right around the bulkhead for the last part of the flight (no meals to serve anymore). She introduced herself and said, "I overheard what you were saying to that young Indian businessman. I am a Christian but I have not been living like one. I never share my faith in Christ with others. Would you pray for me that I will begin to live for Christ and speak freely of Him?" Just around the bulkhead, with my back to the passengers, I offered up a quick prayer specifically for this young lady in these two areas. Her countenance seemed to change at that very moment.

I love these captive audiences: we have full planes with no place to go, no empty seats where they might move and opening the door to leave is not an option.

I said goodbye to her and to Raul as we deplaned and went on my way. I spoke at the missions conference, and five days later, I was headed back home. I was standing in line at the Southwest gate for my flight to San Antonio when an older couple came walking up to me and said, "We remember you from the last flight." I was surprised and asked them why. They said, "We are Christians and we were sitting right behind you as you were sharing Christ with that young Indian business-man. We heard most of what you were saying to him. We were praying for you and for him."

I want to believe that when we are gathered in glory and singing praises to the Lamb with that innumerable throng in Revelation 5 that Raul and his family will be among them.

I was reenergized in my boldness to share the Gospel and to trust in the power of the Holy Spirit to work in ways that we cannot comprehend.

A SECULAR ENVIRONMENTAL SCIENTIST

I boarded the plane, getting a bulkhead seat, and curled up next to the window with a Southwest flight blanket. I was not feeling well. I was running a fever, had a very sore throat, and really didn't care about conversation with anybody. I wanted to be left alone. That was enough witnessing for one trip. But God had other plans.

In came Phil and sat next to the aisle with a vacant seat in between the two of us. So I had some space. We introduced ourselves. He was a great conversationalist. I asked him what he did by way of profession. He told me that he was an environmental scientist. I discovered that he had degrees from Penn State and USC. He was not a fluke. He was a well-educated man. I asked him one question, which led to about a thirty-minute answer. The question was this: "Phil, what do you believe about the future of this planet?" This question was right up his alley. He was well prepared to answer. It was obvious that he had some very strong and well thought-out opinions. He and a number of his colleagues believe that we are living near the end of life on this planet as we know it. He cited the heating up of the core of the earth, global warming, the melting of the ice caps, the rising sea waters, and numerous signals that tell these scientists that we are on a course that, unless reversed, will lead to a catastrophe. He mentioned the "geophysical switch" that he and others believe may happen within our lifetimes. I had never heard of this before and admitted this to him. He explained that it is when the North Pole and the South Pole switch places. It supposedly happens every 30–50,000 years and could be about to happen again. He had no hope for the planet. This scientist was almost overwhelmed by despair, yet intent on doing what he could do to reverse the problem of global warming.

He then asked me what I thought about the future of this planet (I would have asked him to ask me if he hadn't). Even though I was not feeling well, I was feeling good about the question and good about the answers that I had to give to him.

I took him back to the beginning of time and how after God had finished His creative work, He took one look at it and, as it is recorded in Genesis 1:31, we read, "Then God saw everything that he had made, and indeed it was very good. So the evening and the morning were the sixth day" (NKJV). After each act of creation, He pronounced it good, but now He looked at it all collectively and concluded that it was not just good, but "very good."

Continuing, I explained that when God created man He created him with a free will. And that free will of man led to the problems that we now face on this planet. In Genesis 3, Adam and Eve chose to disobey God and, in their rebellion, brought a curse upon mankind. Every man's life goes through the same endless cycles of birth, sin, suffering, and death. It is all because of the curse. And even the woman travails in the moments leading up to childbirth, all because of sin and the curse.

He listened intently as I explained how God provided a cure for sin and how He removes the curse of sin and how, through Christ, we can experience righteousness and life (Romans 5:12–21). I spoke of the crucifixion of Christ and how God placed upon Him the sin of each and every one of us (Isaiah 53:5–7). Three days later, He was raised from the dead. Forty days later, He ascended into the heavens, and He is coming again in power and glory to rescue us from this sin cursed planet at the end of this present age.

His point about how the inner core of the earth is heating up and will make life unbearable on this planet was not forgotten. I brought out II Peter 3 and how God promised that He would never again destroy the earth by a flood (water) but rather by fire. The core of the earth is like a liquid lake of fire and a burning caldron. I quoted II Peter 3:8 to him, "But the heavens and the earth which are now preserved by the same word, are reserved for fire until the Day of Judgment and perdition of ungodly men" (NKJV). And then I quoted verse 10, where Peter writes: "But the day of the Lord will come as a thief in the night, in which the heavens will pass away with a great noise, and the elements will melt with a fervent heat; both the earth and the works that are in it will be burned up" (NKJV).

At this point my new academic acquaintance looked at me and startled me with these words: "By golly, I believe that you are on to something." Isn't that great? Phil never trusted Christ on that flight, but he clearly heard the Gospel. He was encouraged by the hopefulness in the message. He promised me that he would read Andy Stanley's little book. He even said that he would have his wife read it. He said that she was a Roman Catholic, but not practicing her faith. He also promised that he would begin reading the Bible.

As we touched down in Houston and were about to disembark, I stood to my feet. He stood to his and put a hand on my shoulder and said, "You just keep right on doing what you are doing, because by golly, I believe that you are on to something."

OLDER AND BOLDER

It is amazing that God would use a banker from India and a secular scholar from the halls of academia to encourage me to keep on running and keep on sharing Christ. There is no power like the power of the Gospel message. This is why Paul wrote, "For I am not ashamed of the gospel of Christ for it is the power of God unto salvation for everyone who believes, for the Jew first and also for the Greek" (Romans 1:16).

As I get older I want to get bolder. Paul wrote several books while in prison. Ephesians was one of them. At the end of that short letter, he asks them to pray for him. It might not be what you guess. It is not a prayer for deliverance, but rather a prayer for clarity and boldness. He wanted the boldness to speak up for Christ and the clarity to make the Gospel clear to those who would hear. Older and bolder. May that be the theme for each one of us.

Pastor, you hold in your grip the most powerful weapon available to man. It is the power of the Gospel. Don't get discouraged. You just keep on preaching that Word. Keep on doing what you are doing. Keep on running. Crossing that finish line and seeing the Savior will make it all worthwhile.

There hath not failed one word.
This is God's promise to you.
Not a single word of the Word of
God will ever be found untrue.
There will not fail one word. It can-
not happen, my friend.
Not one single syllable God has said
will be less than "yea, and amen."

You can bank your life upon it, though
the winds of affliction assail.
Your life is secure in the hands of a God
whose word simply cannot fail![41]

CHAPTER SIXTEEN
MOTIVATION FOR MINISTRY
ACTS 1:1–11

We live in the hometown of the San Antonio Spurs, the National Basketball Champions in the years 1999, 2003, 2005, and 2007. I am an avid fan. Basketball has always been my favorite sport. I liked almost everything about the Spurs, their character, teamwork, and chemistry. They were a no-nonsense team. This could probably explain why the national news media was not so fond of them. There was, to say it plainly, not enough flash or controversy.

One of the key words in sports these days is the word "motivation." The reason for losses, according to most losing coaches and players, is frequently summed up in this way: a lack of focus, determination, or motivation. You can have all of the credentials, but without motivation, you will not come out on top. In fact, without motivation you will not be able to finish well. We all know of men and women with exceptional gifts who lacked motivation and never lived up to their potential, or simply lost their will to stay in the game or in the marathon.

Quite frankly, there are some days when I just do not feel motivated. As I sat at my computer to write this book there were days when I was more motivated than others. Motivation is something that we all struggle with.

We see a major difference with the disciples between the Gospels and the book of Acts. The major difference is in their courage and motivation. Before His crucifixion, they all fled and scattered away from Him. Following His resurrection and the sending of His Spirit, they were willing to die for Him. What was the difference? Motivation.

What are the motivating factors behind all ministries? I submit to you that the threefold answer is right here in the opening verses of the book of Acts. Our problem is not that we do not know these things, but rather, that we often forget to implement them.

Paul, the seasoned pastor, was writing to a young pastor named Timothy. In II Timothy 2:1–8, he encourages Timothy to be strong in the grace that is in Christ Jesus. He then speaks of the Christian life as being like that of a soldier, an athlete, and a farmer. Each one of these occupations requires discipline, hard work, and motivation in order to succeed. But then he writes: "Remember that Jesus Christ, of the seed of David, was raised from the dead according to my gospel" (II Timothy 2:8, NKJV).

Is it possible to forget that we serve a risen Savior? Evidently it is or Paul would not have challenged Timothy to remember the facts.

Two elderly women were together one day. They had been lifelong friends. But at that particular moment the one lady said to the other, "You know, we have been friends since childhood. We have done many things together. We have traveled together and eaten together and had many experiences together. But for the life of me, I cannot remember your name."

Her elderly friend gave her a rather blank stare for a moment and responded, "Well, do you have to know right now, or can you give me a moment?"

Memory does begin to wane as we get older. If we are not careful, the very things that motivated us in our earlier years of ministry might no longer be in our memory bank, and this may be the reason for lack of motivation.

Luke is writing to set the record straight concerning the facts of the life and ministry of Jesus. He makes reference to the former account in verse 1, which was the book of Luke. He is writing to an individual named Theophilus. We know little about this man. We do know that Luke traveled with Paul in his missionary journeys. Theophilus was probably a young Greek and perhaps a new convert to Christianity, whom Luke had met along the way and was now explaining the facts concerning the Christian faith.

Someone suggested years ago that Theophilus received his name at his moment of birth. When his father first laid eyes on him he lamented, "That's the-awful-lest looking baby I have ever seen." So they called him "The-oph-ilus."

That has nothing to do with the origin of his name. His name comes from a compound Greek word "Theos" and "philos," meaning "God-lover." He was a lover of God. This man had great potential to impact many with the Gospel, but he needed to know the facts.

Luke himself was a very careful historian who was also a medical doctor. He kept detailed records. He gives more insight in his gospel regarding the birth of Christ, the crucifixion, and His resurrection than the other three Gospel writers.

What are the facts that should motivate us?

THE RESURRECTION OF JESUS

Our first motivation for ministry is the resurrection of the Lord Jesus (Acts 1:1–3). The civil and religious authorities counted Jesus down and out. His own followers considered Him to be history. But three days later the tomb was empty. Jesus Christ was alive. During the forty days that intervened between His resurrection and His ascension, according to verse 3, He "proved Himself to be alive by many infallible proofs," and then He was gone.

But He could not leave them until they were fully convinced that He was alive. He suffered and died but then presented Himself to be alive. He did so with compelling evidences. One Greek authority renders this: "In logic: demonstrative proof. In medical language: demonstrative evidence."[42]

Any medical doctor who is to be trusted will not go solely by the way you feel. The doctor will not give a clear diagnosis until he or she has run all the tests. He or she will probably want some X-rays, CAT scans, blood tests, and any number of other modern-day diagnostic procedures to be done. Luke, the physician, would have referred to these as demonstrative evidences.

What were some of these demonstrative evidences? In John 20, Jesus appeared to the disciples, with Thomas present this time, and spoke to Thomas these words: "Reach your finger here, and look at my hands; and reach your hand here and put it into my side. Do not be unbelieving, but believing" (John 20:27, NKJV).

Another case in point, sighted by Luke, probably of the same account, comes in Luke 24:

> Now as they said these things, Jesus Himself stood in the midst of them, and said to them, "Peace

to you." But they were terrified and frightened, and supposed they had seen a spirit. And He said to them, "Why are you troubled? And why do doubts arise in your hearts? Behold my hands and My feet, that it is I Myself. Handle Me and see, for a spirit does not have flesh and bones as you see I have." ["Don't be upset, and don't let all these doubting questions take over. Look at my hands; look at my feet—it's really me. Touch me. Look me over from head to toe. A ghost doesn't have muscle and bone like this." MSG] When He had said this He showed them His hands and His feet. But while they still did not believe for joy, and marveled, He said to them, "Have you any food here?" So they gave Him a piece of a broiled fish and some honeycomb. And He took it and ate in their presence.

Luke 24:36–43 (NKJV)

Jesus appealed to all of their physical senses: hearing, sight, touch, taste, and even their smell.

Christianity is based upon solid historical facts and not mere feelings. He wanted no lingering doubts among them. He wanted them to be fully convinced that He was alive through each of these encounters during the forty days.

He was "being seen by them" (Acts 1:3). Literally, they "eyeballed" Him. They eyeballed him for the forty days.

Back during my seminary days, I began to feel a weakness that grew progressively worse until eventually I was diagnosed with Addison's disease. It severely impaired my metabolism. The doctor who diagnosed it had been a student at Georgetown University Medical School during the time that Kennedy was president. Medical students and doctors in the Washington area were all familiar with Kennedy's Addison's disease in case they ever needed to treat him in an emergency. The doctor asked me a few questions, looked at my discolored skin, checked my vital signs, and wrote down his diagnosis as Addison's disease, or adrenal insufficiency. They put me in the hospital to further test me and confirm that this was the proper diagnosis. This was followed by the prognosis that I would live a normal life, but I would have to take hydrocortisone the rest of my life.

I was just a poor seminary student, with no way to pay our medical bills, which could have been substantial with three major hospitalizations within a year. My doctor had mercy on me and told me that he would forgive the bill if I would come to one of their monthly meetings in which they examine rare diseases and allow nearly forty doctors to go over my body from head to toe. I attended and they eyeballed me for thirty minutes or so.

Not only did Jesus prove Himself to be alive, but He also spoke of matters concerning the Kingdom of God.

There is no way to understand the book of Acts apart from the resurrection of Christ. The NASA space shuttle provides an analogy. It is launched from a platform. It is empowered by fuel, and it has a mission to complete. The disciples are launched out on to a mission in the book of Acts. Their platform was the death and resurrection of Christ. They are empowered on their mission by the Holy Spirit.

Paul builds on these great foundational truths in Romans 1:4, where he speaks of Christ and states that He was "declared [which gives us our English word "horizon"] to be the Son of God with power according to the Spirit of holiness, by the resurrection from the dead" (NKJV). The horizon is a clear boundary. The resurrection of Christ establishes a clear boundary between Himself and all others.

It has been said that people flock to Red Square in Moscow to see the tomb where the body of Lenin lies. But they go to Jerusalem to visit a tomb which the body of Jesus only temporarily occupied. You can name all of the tombs of the great historical political and religious leaders and discover that their tombs are occupied. But the tomb of Jesus has been and remains empty.

The English scholar John Stott has made reference to the fact that the greatest singular evidence for the resurrection of Christ is the changed lives of His followers.

THE SENDING OF HIS HOLY SPIRIT

His resurrection serves as incredible motivation for ministry. But there is a second motivation and that is the sending of His Holy Spirit (Acts 1:4–8). They were commanded to remain in Jerusalem until the Holy Spirit came. In Luke 24:49, Jesus commissioned them, "Behold, I send the Promise of My Father upon you; but tarry in the city of Jerusalem until you are endued with power from on high" (NKJV).

No matter how much we know or how many academic degrees we may have or whatever other resources we might have at our disposal, we are not equipped to go and share such a wonderful message without the power that the Holy Spirit provides us. No amount of preparation and programming can take the place of the Holy Spirit.

You may remember the joke about the college student who bought a chainsaw and used it for several days before he took it back to the dealer. He complained that he could only saw a half of a cord of wood per day.

But the dealer had promised him far more in his sales pitch.

The dealer took the saw in his hands, made a couple of adjustments, pulled the cord and the engine roared into action. The excited college student shouted out, "What's that noise?"

Toward the end of his life, my father-in-law, who, like all of us, was becoming more forgetful with each passing year, experienced something similar with an electric chainsaw. He was about to give up on the chainsaw when I checked up on him. I saw his frustration. I followed the electric cord back to its power source and discovered that it wasn't plugged in. Everything was a go with one important, overlooked exception. All the frustration can be spared if there is connection with the power source.

So many Christians are frustrated and intimidated when trying to share the Gospel with nonbelievers, often because they are trying to do it in their own strength rather than relying upon the Spirit to give clarity and boldness in witness. Pastors burn out and blow out of the ministry by trying to carry the burdens and the weight of the church in their own strength. Even the godly man Moses lost his way in Numbers 11. The complaints of the people had driven him to the end of himself. He begins to assume the ministry as his own.

He cries out, "I am not able to bear all these people alone, because the burden is too heavy for me" (Numbers 11:14, NKJV). Verse 15 further states that he would rather be dead than try to continue in this state. How many pastors and Christian leaders are reading these words and finding themselves similarly burdened down? Maybe it is time to go back to the drawing board. God never intended for the ministry to be yours and for the burden to be put on your back.

Lights will not do what they were intended to do if there is no power. As Christians, we cannot be what God intended us to be apart from His divine power, the indwelling and enabling power of His Spirit.

In the Upper Room Discourse in John 14, Jesus said:

> And I will pray the Father, and He will give you another Helper that He may abide with you forever, the Spirit of truth, whom the world cannot receive, because it neither sees Him, nor knows Him; but you know Him, for He dwells with you and will be in you. I will not leave you orphans; I will come to you.
>
> John 14:16–18 (NKJV)

Reportedly, Dr. Harry Ironside would illustrate the difference between having the Spirit with them, compared to in them. He would use a big, delicious steak to illustrate his point. He would picture it in front of his audience as they were about to cut into this mouth-watering piece of meat. He would then ask them if they would rather have the steak with them or in them.

Jesus was saying to them, in the words of the old American Express credit card advertisement, "Don't leave home without it." Don't leave Jerusalem without His Spirit's presence dwelling in you. The baptism of John was only a ritual, a picture of that which Christ was to do when the Spirit came. We have been to Israel six different times and each time we have baptized people. For many, it is the highlight of the trip. But I will frequently remind them that the greater baptism is not by water, but rather being baptized in His Spirit, being placed into Christ and Christ taking up residence within us. To be immersed in water is one thing. To be immersed in His Spirit is another. You may never make it to the Jordan River to be baptized, but you can enjoy the Spirit's presence wherever you are and wherever you go.

Notice in Acts 1:6 that the disciples are anticipating that this might be the time when God will restore the political and spiritual kingdom to Israel. God isn't finished with Israel yet. God has a plan for His people, the chosen descendants of Abraham. But this was not the time. They wanted the glory days under David and Solomon to return. Jesus answered them in a very gentle way in verse 7. He told them that it was none of their business. It was not for them to know all of the chronological details (times) and the character or circumstances of the times (seasons). Those remain in the jurisdiction of the Father.

But rather, in verse 8, they would receive power and become witnesses unto the uttermost part of the earth. As many have observed, this becomes the outline of the book of Acts.

They were not to be preoccupied with His coming, but rather occupied with their going. And as they went, they were to go in the presence and power of the Holy Spirit. I find myself becoming more and more aware of my own inadequacy in representing Him well to others. Yet at the same time, I am discovering a "holy" boldness as I have opportunity to speak of Him wherever I might be. As mentioned, some of my most productive times of sharing Christ are one-on-one in airplanes. Most of the time, I simply sow the seed of His Word. But every now and then, I get to reap the harvest from someone else's seed that has already been sown. But remember, according to John 4:36, both the one who sows and the one who reaps will rejoice together in heaven.

History bears out that the early followers blanketed

the Roman Empire with the Gospel. Tertullian, an African apologist and theologian between 160–215 a.d., wrote "the outcry is that the state is filled with Christians, that they are in the fields; in the cities, people of both sexes, every age and status, even those of high rank, are passing over to the profession of the Christian faith."

The early followers of Christ were truly inspired to carry the Gospel of Christ to the outer reaches of the Roman Empire, having been motivated by the realization that He is alive and He is present with them through His Holy Spirit.

THE SECOND COMING OF JESUS CHRIST

The final motivation is the second coming of Jesus Christ (Acts 1:9–11). Notice that He was taken up before them into a cloud. He had a cloud waiting for him. When He came into this world, He was wrapped in swaddling clothes. When He exited this world He was enveloped in a cloud of glory, the Shekinah glory, perhaps the same cloud that stood above the people of Israel in the wilderness and rested over the tabernacle and later the temple.

The eleven were straining to keep Him in focus until He was out of sight. It was probably a troubled look of bewilderment as they were trying to grasp the meaning of all of this.

> And while they looked steadfastly toward heaven as He went up, behold, two men stood by them in white apparel, who also said, "Men of Galilee, why do you stand gazing up into heaven? This same Jesus, who was taken up from you into heaven, will so come in like manner as you saw Him go into heaven."
>
> Acts 1:10–11 (NKJV)

"He will return someday in the same manner that He departed on that day. He will descend just as he ascended. He went to heaven and He shall return from heaven. He ascended bodily and He will return bodily. He was taken up visibly, and His return will be visible. He was caught up in a cloud and He will return in the clouds."

In Matthew 24, we hear Jesus say:

Immediately after the tribulation of those days the sun will be darkened, and the moon will not give its light; the stars will fall from heaven, and the powers of the heavens will be shaken. Then the sign of the Son of Man will appear in heaven, and then all the tribes of the earth will mourn, and they will

see the Son of Man coming on the clouds of heaven
with power and great glory.

Matthew 24:29–30 (NKJV)

In Matthew 26:63–64, as Jesus was tried before the Sanhedrin, the high priest demanded, "Tell us if you are the Christ, the Son of God!" Jesus said to him, "It is as you said. Nevertheless, I say to you, hereafter you will see the Son of Man sitting at the right hand of the Power, and coming on the clouds of heaven" (NKJV).

Of course, the theme of the book of Revelation is the unveiling (apokalupsis) of Jesus Christ. In Revelation 1:7 we read, "Behold, He is coming with clouds, and every eye will see Him, even they who pierced Him. And all the tribes of the earth will mourn because of Him. Even so, Amen" (NKJV).

It might be debated whether Christians are caught up before the tribulation (which I personally believe), or at the end of the tribulation, but one thing is crystal clear and we can all agree on it: His coming at the end of the tribulation period, or at the end of time, will be in the clouds and all will see Him.

I am fearful that in this modern age we have lost sight of the fact that Jesus Christ is coming again in power and great glory. We can take that hope to the bank. We should live each day with the realization that it might be our last; this might be the day.

As pastors and leaders we must keep on running, fighting, working, and waiting with our eyes toward that harvest. James 5:7–8 reminds us that we are to "be patient, brethren, until the coming of the Lord. See how the farmer waits for the precious fruit of the earth, waiting patiently for it until it receives the early and latter rain. You also be patient. Establish your hearts, for the coming of the Lord is at hand [has drawn near]" (NKJV).

I have heard it said that we should live as though the crucifixion of Jesus took place yesterday, His resurrection today, and His second coming as occurring tomorrow. Joseph Stowell, in his book Eternity, tells about a friend of his by the name of Bud Wood who has a home for the mentally handicapped children in Union Grove, Wisconsin. Many of these children have Down syndrome and other mental and physical deficiencies. The staff is constantly sharing with the children about this incredible hope in Christ. One of the major problems that they have is dirty windows. Why is that? Joe's friend, Bud Wood, shared, "You can walk through the hallways and corridors any hour of the day and you will see our precious children standing with noses and faces and hands pressed against the windows looking to see if Christ might be coming back that day to take them home and make them whole."[43]

Dear pastor and wife, and dear Christian leader, "Let us not grow weary while doing good, for in due season we shall reap if we do not lose heart" (Galatians 6:9, NKJV).

"Mission Accomplished!"

Mission Accomplished! Dear Lord, may you say
Those beautiful words on that wonderful day,
When into thy presence in heavenly skies,
By grace we behold the love in your eyes.

And listen intently to hear from the Son,
Those priceless of words, "My
child, twas well done."
Oh, the great joy to behold thy dear face
And know in our hearts that we finished the race.
To come to the end and feel no remorse;
To have never looked back to question the course.
To know that the temple our Lord had refined
Was fit for the King for whom it was designed.

To know that tho'oft'times was bitter the cup,
The call of the Master was, "Child, don't give up."
To know at the root of the Saviour's dear heart
Were the words, "Child, just fin-
ish whatever you start."

We were to complete the course he had drawn

Though our spirits grew tired, we were to go on;
Faithful and steadfast, consistent and true,
Remaining devoted till all life was through.

Oh, God, may we hear from your lips on that day
Those words of rejoicing none other can say,
As we flee to thine arms and fall at thy feet:
"Mission Accomplished! Journey Complete!"[44]

EPILOGUE—TRANSITION

My transition from senior pastor at Wayside Chapel to our present ministry with Shepherds' Support, Inc. began back in the fall of 2002. I sensed that God was leading me to begin the transition process. I had seen other churches do it poorly. We wanted our transition to be a model to follow for churches everywhere. So I wrote a letter to our board of elders, giving some timelines. I felt that it would be good if we could have somebody in place by 2005 who could eventually replace me. Once he arrived, for the next two or three years I would still be preaching, less each year. And he would preach more, until I eventually phased out and went full time into encouraging pastors and wives everywhere.

But at the same time, we had personnel issues involving other pastors on staff that took them away from Wayside, and we put the announcing of my departure on hold until January of 2005. We prepared the congregation by simply stating that we were beginning the search for a new senior pastor. We also told them that we were not going anywhere. We would continue to minister there and be involved with the people. We had been there thirty-three years at that point. We did not give any definite date for our departure.

Then, in January of 2006, in my state of the church address, I gave the date to be the first of June in 2006.

That was when the church honored Connie and me with a weekend celebration. I wanted Pastor Rander Draper and his wife, Darlene, of Maranatha Bible Church, our dear friends, to be the ones sharing that weekend with us. Pastor Rander spoke in all three weekend services. We have ministered together in many different countries since the early 1990s, as well as exchanged pulpits each year.

Meanwhile, the church had a search committee in place, and they were beginning to narrow their search in the middle of that summer. They ended up selecting Dr. Roger Poupart and his wife, Kim. He has been an excellent choice as my replacement. He has honored us on a regular basis by referring to our legacy of the past thirty-four years, and he has made it much easier for us to be there and even be involved. So Wayside Chapel continues to be our home church and supports us in its monthly missions budget. We could not have asked for a better situation. We have also tried to remain low-key so as not to take away from Roger and Kim as they put their roots down here. We pray for a long and productive ministry for them, just as we enjoyed.

Sometime in the early part of my transition, I read Bob Buford's latest book, Finishing Well.[45] It was very helpful and encouraging to me personally. In the book he interviews a number of successful people who had changed course around the age of sixty, which was my age in 2003, and transitioned into causes that they were passionate about. He builds his premise around the perspective that you spend the first forty years of your adult life doing the things that you have to do in order to spend the last twenty or thirty years doing the things that you really enjoy doing. I love to preach and teach and disciple and encourage others. But I increasingly found the administrative and personnel issues to be a burden to me. These kept me from doing well what I do best and what God created and gifted me to do.

God was building a passion in my life for developing Christian leaders around the world. I had already spoken at a number of conferences from east to west. Our missions pastor, Marvin Smith, and others, kept hearing reports about how much these leaders received through our ministry. This confirmed in us the calling that we felt God was giving to us. We owe much to Marvin's encouragement and strategic thinking. He went to be with the Lord in January of 2006, following a long battle with cancer. It was fitting that Connie and I were ministering in Northern India at the time, to 1,600 church planters and pastors, serving alongside evangelist Sammy and Tex Tippit. Georgette, Marvin's wife, and the rest of the family waited for us to return so I could speak at his memorial service. God greatly used him during his ten years on our staff as well as his wisdom given to us during our transition.

At our retirement celebration, many colleagues said some nice things about us, including Max Lucado. Max, at that time, gave me his latest book, which he signed, entitled Cure for the Common Life. In chapter 1, entitled "Your Sweet Spot (You Have One!)," he writes:

> "Sweet spot." Golfers understand the term. So do tennis players. Ever swung a baseball bat or paddled a Ping-Pong ball? If so, you know the oh-so-nice feel of the sweet spot. Connect with these prime inches of real estate and kapow! The collective technologies of the universe afterburn the ball into orbit, leaving you Frisbee-eyed and strutting. Your arm doesn't tingle, and the ball doesn't ricochet. Your boyfriend remembers birthdays, the tax refund comes early, and the flight attendant bumps you up to first class. Life in the sweet spot rolls like the downhill side of a downwind bike ride.[46]

He then goes on to state that God has given each one of us a sweet spot and life makes more sense when we are operating within it.

We feel that we have found our sweet spot in which we can function as long as God calls us to do it and provides for our needs.

I would be remiss if I did not mention another very important part of our transition. We have a team without which we could not do what we are doing. In the fall of 2005, we put together a team consisting of four other couples, John and Marsha Shields, Doctors Keith and Beth Eyre, Lannie and Melba Green, and Dr. Glen and Marilyn Mott. They have furnished much-needed encouragement, wisdom, and accountability. We have been blessed and helped immensely by each one of these board members. We regularly thank and praise God for them. We are excited about what God has for us in the future.

Since stepping down in June of 2006, we have ministered in pastors' wives conferences in Uganda, Romania, Northern India, Zambia, Rwanda, Croatia, South Africa, Nigeria, and Malawi. We already have six more conferences scheduled for 2009 and 2010, with others in the process.

Paul's passion and ministry in life are an encouragement to me. Romans 1:10–12 have become the theme verses in our ministry. Paul is writing to the Romans, whom he had not yet visited. He writes of his desire to visit them:

One of the things that I always pray for is the opportunity, God willing, to come at last to see you. For I long to visit you so I can bring you some spiritual gift that will help you grow strong in the Lord. When we get together, I want to encourage you in your faith, but I also want to be encouraged by yours.

Romans 1:10–12 (NLT)

Paul's outlook on death also encourages me:

For I am already being poured out as a drink offering, and the time of my departure is at hand. I have fought the good fight, I have finished the race, I have kept the faith. Finally, there is laid up for me the crown of righteousness, which the Lord, the righteous Judge, will give to me on that Day, and not to me only but also to all who have loved His appearing.

II Timothy 4:6–8 (NKJV)

Bob Buford gives us two great questions that He might ask us on that day when we each stand before Him. He writes:

I'm convinced that when I get to heaven and come face-to-face with my Creator, there's going to be a final exam, and as I visualize it, two questions will sum up the part of my life lived on earth: (1) "What did you do about Jesus?" and (2) "What did you do with what I gave you to work with?" One question about belief and one question about action—not action in lieu of belief (the old word is "works") but action that grows out of belief. It's both/and not either/or.[47]

These two questions go well with those asked by the Saul of Tarsus (the apostle Paul) on the road to Damascus when he first met the risen Lord Jesus Christ. He asked, "Who are You, Lord?" and then continues, "Lord, what do You want me to do?" (Acts 9:5–6, NKJV). How about you asking Him those same two questions and see what He says to you?

ENDNOTES

Chapter One: Meet Maria—A Woman of Prayer

1   Richard A. Swenson, M.D. "The Pain of Stress," in Margin: Restoring Emotional, Physical, Financial, and Time Reserves to Overloaded Lives (Colorado Springs, CO: NavPress Publishing Group, 1992), 57–71.

2   Russell Kelfer, Follow Me (San Antonio, TX: Discipleship Tape Ministries, 2001), 105.

Chapter Two: Who Are You, Really?

3   Brennan Manning, Abba's Child: The Cry of the Heart for Intimate Belonging (Colorado Springs, CO: NavPress Publishing Group, 1994), 99.

4   Bob George, Classic Christianity (Eugene, OR: Harvest House Publishers, 1989), 77–78.

5   John MacArthur, The MacArthur Study Bible (Dallas: Word Publishing, 1997), 1702.

6   W.W. Martin, "The Wilderness Offerings," The Keswick Convention (1930), 172.

Chapter Three: Meet David Allen—A Man of the Word

7   Steve Farrar, Finishing Strong (Portland, OR: Mult-
    nomah Books, 1995), 71.

8   Church Signs 2008 Calendar (Riverside, NJ:
    Andrews McMeel Publishing, LLC, 2008) January.

Chapter Four: Looking unto Jesus

9   Charles W. Price, Christ For Real (Grand Rapids,
    MI: Kregel Publications, 1995), 111–12.

10 Steve Farrar, Finishing Strong, 6–7.

11 Unknown Author, "Donkey Legend."

12 Russell Kelfer, "Finish Well" (San Antonio, TX:
    Discipleship Tape Ministries, 2001).

**Chapter Five: Meet Ray Stedman—A Pastor to Pas-
tors**

15 Mark S. Mitchell, Portrait of Integrity: The Life
    of Ray C. Stedman (Grand Rapids, MI: Discovery
    House Publishers, 2004), 15.

14 Ibid. 199–200.

15 Ibid. 153.

16 Ibid. 168.

17 Ibid. 154.

18 Steve Farrar, Finishing Strong, 13.

Chapter Six: The Way Up Is Down

19 Max Lucado, Cure for the Common Life: Living in Your Sweet Spot (Nashville, TN: W Publishing Group, 2005), 87–88.

20 Stuart Briscoe, Bound for Joy: A Bible Commentary for Laymen (Ventura, CA: Regal Books, 1975), 73.

21 Mike Yankoski, Under the Overpass (Portland, OR: Multnomah Books, 2005).

22 Author Unknown, "The Judgment Seat of Christ."

Chapter Seven: Meet Russell Kelfer—"Not I, But Christ"

23 The Keswick Convention (1931), 168.

24 Russell Kelfer, Follow Me, 58–59.

Chapter Eight: It's All About Him

25 Brennan Manning, Ruthless Trust (New York: HarperSanFrancisco, 2000), 49.

26 Ray Price, "How Big Is God."

Chapter Nine: Meet Bill Cose—A Man of Faith and Encouragement

27 Russell Kelfer, "The Battle is Not Yours," Follow Me, 40–41.

Chapter Ten: We Are At War

28 Lt. Gen. Romeo Dallaire, Shake Hands with the Devil (New York: Carroll & Graf Publishers, 2003), 24–25.

29 William Gurnall, The Christian in Complete Armor (Carlisle, PA: Banner of Truth, 1986), 1:140–41.

30 Martin Luther, "A Mighty Fortress Is Our God," Stanza 1.

31 Chief Iron Eyes Cody, in a lecture he would give to high school students regarding the danger of drugs.

32 Russell Kelfer, "Hath God Said?" Until He Comes Again, 109.

Chapter Eleven: Meet an Unknown Preacher in Northern Burma

33 Russell Kelfer, "Reaching Out Together" (San Antonio, TX: Discipleship Tape Ministries, 2001).

Chapter Twelve: Giving Him All You Have

34 Fritz Rienecker and Cleon Rogers, Linguistic Key to the Greek New Testament (New York: Zondervan, 1976), 175.

35 S.D. Gordon, "Christ's Promise of Rest," The Keswick Convention (1931), 135–36.

36 Lois Dehoff and Evelyn Baer, "May Christ Be Seen in Me," Sacred Songs (Waco, TX: 1965).

Chapter Thirteen: Meet a Forgiving Translator in Romania

37 Lindsay Glegg, "The Autobiography of a Christian," The Keswick Convention (1931), 69–74.

38 The White Sisters, "Yes, He Did!" (Singspiration, 1954).

Chapter Fourteen: Abiding in Christ

39 Russell Kelfer, "Teach Me to Abide," Until He Comes Again, 9.

Chapter Fifteen: Meet a Banker, A Stewardess, and an Environmental Scientist

40 Andy Stanley, How Good Is Good Enough? (Portland OR: Multnomah Books, 2003).

41 Russell Kelfer, "There Hath Not Failed One Word," Until He Comes Again, 119.

Chapter 16: Motivation for Ministry

42 Fritz Rienecker and Cleon Rogers, Linguistic Key, 263.

43 Joseph Stowell, Eternity: Reclaiming a Passion for What Endures (Chicago: Moody Press, 1995) 122.

44 Russell Kelfer, "Mission Accomplished," Until He Comes Again, 156–57.

Epilogue—Transition Time

45 Bob Buford, Finishing Well (Mobile, AL: Integrity Publishers, 2004).

46 Max Lucado, Cure for the Common Life, 1.

47 Bob Buford, Finishing Well, 171.

BIBLIOGRAPHY

Briscoe, Stuart. Bound for Joy: A Bible Commentary for Laymen. Ventura, CA: Regal Books, 1975.

Buford, Bob. Finishing Well. Mobile, AL: Integrity Publishers, 2004.

Cody, Iron Eyes. Lecture to high school students on drugs

Dallaire, Lt. Gen. Romeo. Shake Hands with the Devil. New York: Carroll & Graf Publishers, 2003.

Dehoff, Lois and Evelyn Baer. "May Christ Be Seen in Me." Sacred Songs. Waco, TX: 1965.

Farrar, Steve. Finishing Strong. Portland, OR: Multnomah Books, 1995.

George, Bob. Classic Christianity. Eugene, OR: Harvest House Publishers, 1989.

Glegg, Lindsay. "The Autobiography of a Christian." The Keswick Convention, 1931.

Gordon, S.D. "Christ's Promise of Rest." The Keswick Convention, 1931.

Gurnall, William. The Christian in Complete Armor. Vol. 1. Carlisle, PA: Banner of Truth, 1986.

Kelfer, Russell. "Finish Well." San Antonio, TX: Discipleship Tape Ministries, 2001.

Kelfer, Russell. Follow Me. San Antonio, TX: Discipleship Tape Ministries, 2001.

Kelfer, Russell. "Reaching Out Together." San Antonio, TX: Discipleship Tape Ministries, 2001.

Kelfer, Russell. Until He Comes Again. San Antonio, TX: Discipleship Tape Ministries, 2001.

Lucado, Max. Cure for the Common Life: Living in Your Sweet Spot. Nashville, TN: W Publishing Group, 2005.

Luther, Martin. "A Might Fortress Is Our God."

MacArthur, John A. The MacArthur Study Bible. Dallas: Word Publishing, 1997.

Manning, Brennan. Abba's Child: The Cry of the Heart for Intimate Belonging. Colorado Springs, CO: NavPress Publishing Group, 1994.

Manning, Brennan. Ruthless Trust. New York: HarperSanFrancisco, 2000.

Martin, W.W. "The Wilderness Offerings." The Keswick Convention, 1930.

Mitchell, Mark S. Portrait of Integrity: The Life of Ray

C. Stedman. Grand Rapids, MI: Discovery House Publishers, 2004.

Price, Charles W. Christ For Real. Grand Rapids, MI: Kregel Publications, 1995.

Rienecker, Fritz and Cleon Rogers. Linguistic Key to the Greek New Testament. New York: Zondervan, 1976.

Sproul, R.C. The Holiness of God. Carol Stream, IL: Tyndale Publishers, 1985.

Stanley, Andy. How Good Is Good Enough? Portland, OR: Multnomah Books, 2003.

Stowell, Joseph. Eternity: Reclaiming a Passion for What Endures. Chicago: Moody Press, 1995.

Stowell, Joseph. "Strength for the Journey." Not Quite Dead. Podcast, 12 June 2007.

Swenson, Richard A. M.D. "The Pain of Stress." In Margin: Restoring Emotional, Physical, Financial, and Time Reserves to Overloaded Lives. Colorado Springs: Navpress Publishing Group, 1992.

Unknown Author. "Donkey Legend."

Unknown Author. "The Judgment Seat of Christ."

White Sisters, The. "Yes, He Did!" Singspiration, 1954.

Yankoski, Mike. Under the Overpass. Portland, OR: Multnomah Books, 2005.